THE
BROWN'S
CHICKEN
MASSACRE

MAURICE POSSLEY

BERKLEY BOOKS, NEW YORK

"The mystery of a terrible destiny will live on in Palatine," written by Eugene Kennedy, published January 15, 1983, and January 19, 1983 copyright © 1983 Chicago Tribune Company. All rights reserved. Used with permission.

THE BROWN'S CHICKEN MASSACRE

A Berkley Book / published by arrangement with
the author

PRINTING HISTORY
Berkley edition / August 2003

Copyright © 2003 by Maurice Possley
Cover design by Steve Ferlauto
Text design by Kristin del Rosario

For information address: The Berkley Publishing Group,
a division of Penguin Group (USA) Inc.,
375 Hudson Street, New York, New York 10014.

ISBN: 0-425-19085-4

BERKLEY®
Berkley Books are published by The Berkley Publishing Group,
a division of Penguin Group (USA) Inc.,
375 Hudson Street, New York, New York 10014.
BERKLEY and the "B" design
are trademarks belonging to Penguin Group (USA) Inc.

PRINTED IN THE UNITED STATES OF AMERICA

10 9 8 7 6 5 4 3

For
Richard Ehlenfeldt
Lynn Ehlenfeldt
Guadalupe Maldonado
Michael Castro
Thomas Mennes
Rico Solis
Marcus Nellsen
and
their families

ACKNOWLEDGMENTS

I am grateful to many for their assistance in this endeavor. For her patience and support, I thank my wife, Cathleen Falsani. For suggesting this book and for her careful attention to the manuscript, I thank my editor, Martha Bushko. I am thankful for the wisdom of my agent, Rafael Sagalyn. For her excellent research, I am very thankful to Sharon Barrett.

In particular, I owe a debt of gratitude that can never be paid (and thankfully, he will never try to collect) to Rick Kogan, my colleague, collaborator, and dear friend of more than twenty-five years.

This book could not have come to life without the many hours of work of the many reporters that labored on the story for nearly a decade at the *Chicago Tribune,* the *Chicago Sun-Times,* the *Daily Herald,* the *Daily Southtown,* Copley Press, the Associated Press, and other news-gathering organizations. Undoubtedly, I have missed some, though not intentionally.

For their news-gathering efforts, I am grateful to: Jim Allen, Ken Armstrong, Art Barnum, Becky Beaupre, Robert Becker, Lee Bey, Ed Bierschenk, Lisa Black, Phil Borchmann, Angela Bradbery, Karen Brandon, Frank Burgos, Rudolph Bush, John Carpenter, Rebecca Carr, Jim Casey, Sheridan Chaney, Desiree Chen, Sue Ellen Christian, Mickey Ciokajlo, Chris Clair, Cass Cliatt, Jeff

Coen, Sharon Cohen, Burt Constable, Sharon Cotliar, Yvette Craig, Jerry Crimmins, Monica Davey, Sandra Del Re, Tracy Dell'Angela, Stefanie Dell'Aringa, Adrienne Drell, Cliff Edwards, Robert Enstad, Andrew Fegelman, Eric Ferkenhoff, Lee Filas, Scott Fornek, John Fountain, Philip Franchine, Chris Fusco, Freida Gad, Maria T. Galo, Laurie Goering, Art Golab, Veronica Gonzalez, John Gorman, Chuck Goudie, Michael Gougis, William Grady, Ted Gregory, Kate N. Grossman, Ben Grove, William Gruber, Lucio Guerrero, Janan Hanna, Larry Hartstein, V. Dion Haynes, Andrew Hermann, Michael Higgins, Mary Hill, Mary Beth Hoerner, Stanley Holmes, Jack Houston, David Ibata, Julie Irwin, Noah Isaackson, Bechetta Jackson, Laura Janota, Kevin Johnson, Lynette Kalsnes, Shia Kapos, Carri Karuhn, John Kass, Michael Kates, David R. Kazak, John Keilman, Peter Kendall, Louise Kiernan, Joseph Kirby, Steve Kloehn, Natasha Korecki, Karen Cullotta Krause, Eric Krol, Susan Kuczka, Curtis Lawrence, Nancy Lawson, Michael Lev, Terri Ann Lewis, Jeff Long, Ray Long, Frank Main, Jeremy Manier, Dave Mann, Andrew Martin, Mitch Martin, Michael Martinez, Teresa Mask, Tom McCann, Rhoda McKinney, Colin McMahon, Tom McNamee, Flynn McRoberts, Chuck McWhinnie, Bob Merrifield, Dan Mihalopoulos, Sabrina L. Miller, Steve Mills, Robin Mohr, Charles Mount, Dave Newbart, John O'Brien, Phillip J. O'Connor, Chris O'Donnell, Maureen O'Donnell, Tom O'Konowitz, Lou Ortiz, Gene O'Shea, Dave Orrick, Tom Pelton, Lynn Rogers Petrak, Steven Price, Ray Quintanilla, Diane Rado, William Recktenwald, Ginger D. Richardson, Jim Ritter, Michelle Roberts, Alex Rodriguez, James Rowen, Dan Rozek, Martha Russis, Nancy Ryan, Carlos Sadovi, Kathy Sanders, Dave Savini, Rhonda Sciarra, Anika M. Scott, Dionne

Searcey, Jerry Shnay, Mark Shuman, Alf Siewers, David Silverman, Joseph Sjostrom, Bryan Smith, Michael Sneed, Jamie Sotonoff, Kara Spak, Carolyn Starks, Bob Susnjara, Diane Struzzi, Sarah Talalay, Lindsey Tanner, Alysia Tate, Jerry Thomas, Shamus Toomey, Darryl Van Duch, Lyn Van Matre, Matthew Walberg, Steve Warmbir, Mike Waters, Teresa Wiltz, Christine Winter, Gary Wisby, Rogers Worthington, Richard Wronski, Crystal Yednak, David Young, and Eric Zorn.

AUTHOR'S NOTE

Kathleen Parker is a pseudonym used to protect the identity of a witness.

ONE

Y OU WOULD LIKE TO BELIEVE THAT ON THE morning of the day that he would die, Guadalupe Maldonado awoke smiling, that he had dreamed of Mexico again, and that always made him happy, even in his dreams, especially during harsh Midwestern winters.

And so, when he awoke just after 10 A.M. on January 8, 1993, he was smiling. He was not ordinarily a late sleeper, but for the past week he had been working the 1 P.M. to 9 P.M. shift as a cook at Brown's Chicken & Pasta in Palatine, Illinois, a quiet suburb thirty miles northwest of downtown Chicago. He lived only a few miles away, and when he got home, he spent time with his wife, Beatriz, catching up on the activities of the day, especially those of their three children, and did not go to bed until after midnight.

Guadalupe and his family, like generations of immigrants before them, were living out their particular version of the American Dream. At forty-seven, he was not a man of large ambitions. A steady paycheck, a pleasant place in which to work, and a cozy home in which to live were his principal aspirations, and he was well on his way to attaining them. The bigger dreams, the higher hopes, he and his wife were investing in their kids.

The Maldonados had one child and one on the way when they first came to the United States in 1981, settling into the northwest suburbs of Chicago. They had relatives in the area who helped arrange for a place to live. Work was easy to find, and after a series of jobs, most of them in the food service industry, they both were hired to work at Ye Olde Towne Inn, a restaurant and bar in Mt. Prospect, where occasionally rock bands provided entertainment. He cooked. Beatriz cleaned up.

The couple liked that they worked together and they liked life in the United States. Again, like generations of immigrants before them, they tried to aid others in coming to this country, often lending money for the trip to relatives and friends, and then helping them find jobs and homes.

It was with understandable reluctance, then, that Guadalupe and his family returned to Mexico late in 1989. But following his father's death, he and his four brothers inherited a one-and-a-half-acre plot of land and decided that they should take turns farming it while the others went to the United States to work. The plan was that all of them would eventually be able to settle in the States.

They were born to be farmers. Guadalupe, the second eldest of the five boys, was raised in the state of Guanajuato, a rural, mountainous area in central Mexico. It was no longer a wealthy area but historically had been one of Mexico's richest.

The capital of the state of the same name, Guanajuato,

which means "hilly place of frogs," is one of Mexico's most beautifully preserved colonial cities, filled with homes and buildings that indicate its prosperous past. The Spanish discovered silver and gold there in the midfifteenth century, and for two centuries afterward 30 to 40 percent of the world's silver was mined in Guanajuato. Adding to the already eye-pleasing structures left by the Spanish, many other architecturally outstanding monuments and buildings were built in the early twentieth century.

These historic structures, along with the subterranean tunnels, a labyrinth of aboveground alleys called *callejones,* and a mosaic of colorfully painted houses jutting up the sides of the mountains that encircle the city are part of Guanajuato's unique atmosphere. The Maldonados visited the capital infrequently. They stayed mostly on the farm, where their life was neatly summarized by Guadalupe's brother Juan Pablo as one in which "we plant corn and watch it grow."

Their homeland was a beautiful place, becoming increasingly popular with tourists from the United States and Canada. It was an area guidebooks referred to as colorful and charming.

The same could not be said for Palatine, Illinois. Though it was dotted with some fine and handsome homes, it had the homogeneous look of many of the suburbs that surrounded Chicago, suburbs that had witnessed significant growth and change after World War II as the expressway system made them more accessible to city dwellers looking for places where they might escape what they considered the negative aspects of Chicago: racial conflict, slums, high taxes, high land values, congestion, pollution, poor schools, and crime. Palatine, located as it is within miles of the world's busiest airport, was derisively lumped with neighboring suburbs into an amorphous place called the Land Beyond O'Hare.

But in December 1992, Palatine was where Guadalupe and his family moved when they came back from Mexico, taking up residence in the house where his brother Pedro, and Pedro's wife, Juana, lived for what they believed would be a short time before they had enough money to buy a place of their own.

Guadalupe had been eager to return, rejecting the warnings of Pedro, who had spent months writing him letters trying to convince him to stay in Mexico. "You won't recognize the area from when you were last here," Pedro had told his older brother throughout 1992. "Jobs are bad. Things are not the same. It is not as safe. It is getting more dangerous here."

Jobs *were* bad. Guadalupe wasn't able to return to his old position as cook at Ye Olde Towne Inn, though its owners promised that they would bring him back in a few months. He spent some fruitless days searching for work before being hired at Brown's Chicken & Pasta. It was a few days before Christmas and he was happy to have any sort of work. Money was getting tight.

At Christmas, he and his wife could afford to buy only one gift, for their youngest son, five-year-old Salvador. They asked the older boys, thirteen-year-old Juan Pablo and eleven-year-old Javier, to understand the necessity for sacrifice.

On the night of January 8, the kids were asleep but the rest of the family awaited Guadalupe's arrival. He was going to have his first paycheck from Brown's. He was always home by 10 P.M. But this night he was not, and at about 11 P.M. Beatriz called the restaurant. There was no answer.

"He is always home by ten," said Juana. "He calls if he is going to be late."

Just after midnight, Beatriz asked Pedro to drive to the restaurant to check on him. There is no knowing how worried Pedro was as he put on his winter coat and walked to the car, but it's likely that his previous warnings to his brother echoed in his head: "It is not as safe."

The drive to the restaurant didn't take long, and when Pedro pulled into the parking lot, he knew something was wrong. There were three cars parked there, unusual for this time of night. One of them was Guadalupe's. There was no mistaking it. Pedro had given his brother the Dodge Charger a month earlier, shortly after his return from Mexico.

As Pedro wheeled his car around the lot, he heard a noise behind him and turned to see a Palatine police car. He stopped and the squad car pulled up alongside him. The officer signaled him to roll down his window.

"What are you doing here?" asked the officer.

"My brother did not come home from work," said Pedro, his words halting and his accent thick, not confident of his English. "He works in there, at the chicken place."

"He'll be home," the officer said.

"But—" Pedro started to say.

"Now go home," said the officer. "He's probably out drinking or hanging out."

Pedro nodded—he knew better than to argue with the police. But as he rolled up his window, he was filled with fear. His brother was not a drinker. If he had time to "hang out," he preferred to do so with his family.

Pedro drove home. When he walked into the house alone, he could see the worry on the faces of his wife and sister-in-law. He told them what had happened.

"We thought something was very wrong," Juana said.

So sure of that were she and her husband and Beatriz that they roused the children and together they stayed up and waited, hoping for the best, fearing the worst, and trying to imagine scenarios in which Guadalupe was safe.

Had there been some sort of accident?

Not likely, since his car was still in the lot.

Did his car fail to start?

Maybe he had gotten a ride from someone who worked at the restaurant.

Did they have car trouble on the way?

Maybe. Maybe. Maybe.

Some of those same questions were being asked in another part of town. The family of sixteen-year-old Michael Castro had also been worrying for hours after their son failed to come home shortly after the 9 P.M. closing of Brown's. Like Guadalupe, he always called if he was going to be late.

Shortly after 11 P.M., his parents, Emmanuel and Epifania Castro, drove to the restaurant. It was dimly lit and appeared to be closed. A police officer was in his car in the parking lot. He told them not to worry, saying, "He'll come home. He'll be back. He'll call."

The Castros returned home, but at 1 A.M. they called the police again. They wanted to file a missing person's report, and an officer came to their home to fill out the paperwork. But before that task was done, the increasingly worried couple requested to be allowed to return to Brown's. Alone in his car, Michael's father followed the police car to the parking lot. After they arrived and began to closely inspect the building, peering through the windows into the darkened restaurant, Michael's father saw a mop leaning against the wall.

"They wouldn't let these people leave the mop there," he said, the words frantic and fearful. "They'd make them put it in the closet."

Then he noticed another item and shouted, "That's my son's jacket over there!"

He and the officer began checking doors.

The officer found a side door unlocked. "Stay put," he told Emmanuel, and opened the door and peered inside.

A few seconds felt like minutes to Castro, who asked, "What? What is it?" as he started to walk toward the door just as the officer was coming out, saying, his voice quavering, "Back off! There's been a crime committed here."

"Where's my son?" Castro yelled. "Is he hurt?"

TWO

THE CALL SHATTERED THE EARLY MORNING, shocked a city, and would forever haunt those who heard it. Its message was this: "Five in the cooler at Brown's."

The call came at 3:11 A.M. That is the exact time that Palatine police officers Kurt Saxma and Ron Conley let others know via police radio call that they had discovered one of the most gruesome murder scenes in Illinois history.

"Five in the cooler at Brown's."

The "cooler" was actually the store's freezer on the east side of the building. The victims were wearing Brown's Chicken & Pasta uniforms. The uniforms were soaked in blood.

At 3:20 A.M., Palatine police sergeant Bob Haas arrived on the scene. In the west cooler, one of the two rooms in the restaurant where food was stored, he found two more bodies. One was in a Brown's uniform. The other was not. They, too, were covered with blood.

Almost immediately, Palatine police chief Jerry Bratcher called in another agency, the Northern Illinois Police Crime Laboratory, to help collect evidence. Cook County Police were also there, as was the chief investigator for the Cook County State Attorney's Office, Kevin Kavanaugh. By daylight, more than one hundred officers and technicians would be on the scene.

The restaurant's parking lot was soon filled with police cars and ambulances. The crime scene had been secured "narrowly," meaning that only the area closest to the restaurant was confined. Cars carrying reporters and trucks carrying television news crews jammed the parking lot as well. Satellite dishes were raised. And snow began to fall.

The news was spreading fast. Stunned Brown's employees, curiosity seekers, police, fire trucks, ambulances, and reporters filled the lot that surrounded the restaurant, which stood alone at 168 Northwest Highway, about a hundred yards from a strip of stores that composed what was then called the Eagle Plaza Shopping Center. It was a typical suburban commercial complex: grocery store, hairdresser, pet shop, dry cleaner, travel agency, and an armed forces recruiting office.

Seventeen-year-old Casey Sander, one of many teenagers who worked at the restaurant, was listening to the radio at 7 A.M. when she heard the news. She quickly dressed and rode her bicycle to the store. When she arrived, five or six of her fellow workers ran to embrace her. "They were really happy to see me. It was a very strange feeling," Sander told the *Chicago Tribune*. "They thought I was dead, and I thought they were dead."

Jason Georgi was already there. He had taken Friday night off, after asking if someone could fill in for him so that he could go with friends to the homecoming basketball game pitting his Palatine High Pirates against rival Fremd. It was an intense rivalry, with Fremd riding a five-year streak of play-off victories over Palatine, each time ending the Pirates' season. In front of fourteen hundred screaming spectators, Palatine had ended that streak Friday night, winning 50–40. But no one was talking about the game.

"I feel terrible for whoever it was who took my place," Georgi said, standing outside the store. "Any other Friday night, that would be me in there."

Sander pointed to a red car in the parking lot and said aloud that it belonged to seventeen-year-old Rico Solis. "I think he's dead," she said. "He was so quiet and nice. I can't imagine anyone killing him."

Things unimaginable were starting to sink in.

In her nearby home, Evelyn Solis, Rico's mother, demanded that family members take her to the restaurant. They arrived at 10:15 A.M. and the mother immediately became hysterical at the sight of her son's car in the parking lot.

"That's my only son they took," she screamed as she began to sob. "He was just a hardworking guy. Why, Lord, why? I can't take it. I can't take it."

Michael Castro's sister, Mary Jane Crow, was summoned from a cousin's home where she had spent the night. She had worked at the same Brown's restaurant several years earlier under a different franchise owner. Although she was seven years older than Michael, they were very close and she knew that he worked at Brown's three or four days a week, always on the 5 P.M. to 9 P.M.

shift. When she arrived at the police station, very little information was being given out, even to family members.

"But why won't they just tell us?" was a frequent refrain in the parking lot.

The police were not saying anything. That's usually the way it is at a crime scene: the lid is on. And the magnitude of this crime was overwhelming. Inside the restaurant, it was chaos. It even took several minutes for police and firefighters to accurately count the bodies. One paramedic counted eight, but there were actually seven.

Five of the bodies were piled on top of one another in the east freezer: Maldonado, Castro, and Solis, thirty-one-year-old Marcus Nellsen, and forty-nine-year-old Lynn Ehlenfeldt, one of the restaurant's owners.

Her fifty-year-old husband, Richard, was dead in the west cooler, along with thirty-two-year-old Thomas Mennes, the only victim not wearing a Brown's uniform. On that night Mennes was working as a "breader," a job that did not require a uniform because he did not have any contact with the public.

All seven had suffered fatal gunshot wounds to the head, some once, others as many as six times. More than twenty shots had been fired. The victims appeared to have been killed "execution style," since all seven were shot from behind, suggesting that they had been forced to kneel with their backs to the killer or killers.

Some of the victims also bore evidence of having been beaten and knifed. Castro and Solis, it appeared to some investigators, had been singled out for particularly brutal treatment. Each had been shot more than once, and Castro had what appeared to be a number of knife wounds on his torso. Lynn Ehlenfeldt's throat had been cut.

Potential evidence was all over the restaurant. The

bloody mop that the killers apparently had used to clean some of the scene was resting near the east door. The hand of one victim extended out of the doorway of the freezer and bloody prints were on the doorframe. A bullet hole in the ceiling hinted at the firing of a warning or control shot.

The safe still had the key in it.

But just as important as the evidence that was present was the evidence that was absent. Police found no shell casings and the killers had left money on some victims while taking what would eventually be determined to be $1,800 in cash from the safe. Money was found in the sock of one victim and the wallet of another. The credit card of one of the victims was hidden behind some boxes.

Notebooks filled with notations; bags with evidence; the air with theories. The names of Richard Speck and John Wayne Gacy filled the air, as some, grasping clumsily for comparisons to the scene of which they were a part, recalled the names of the area's most notorious killers.

One of the investigators noted, but could not immediately explain why, the face of a wall clock was cracked, the hands frozen at 9:50.

Another investigator checked the cash register. He punched a button and shot out the five-dollar receipt for the last order served Friday night: chicken dinner for one, rolls, and a drink. At the top of the slip was the time—9:08 P.M. An unused drink cup stood undisturbed on the counter.

All day long, people came to and went from the restaurant and the parking lot. The lack of information, of details however grisly, made the entire day even more horrible to those who stood vigil, allowing this crime to develop the black personality of a terrible dream. As the day dragged past noon, many wondered why none of the bodies had been removed.

"Death's snowy cowl only made its visit to the gentle suburb of Palatine more terrible. For there, in as unguarded and ordinary a moment as America knows—closing time in a family-run restaurant on Saturday night—random evil, mocking goodness beneath its shield of invisibility, smashed the lives and dreams of seven people," former priest and author Eugene Kennedy wrote days later in the *Chicago Tribune*. "In this mystery of life and death in Palatine, we may sense secret causes as well. For here was a grouping of people who looked far more like America than President-elect Clinton's arduously chosen cabinet members did. They bore, as well, the strengths and the sorrows, as well as the history and hopes of the nation in their lives."

Such lofty sentiments were not present in the words or thoughts of those who stood freezing in the parking lot. Rather, to fill the information void, there were theories, the most likely being that this was a robbery gone terribly wrong. Others discussed what they believed was the restaurant's vulnerability. Some employees said they had been fearful that something like this would happen, that security was lax.

A rear door was usually left unlocked, with the restaurant's floor safe about eight feet from it. There was usually about $3,000 in the safe and everyone knew that, Georgi told the *Tribune*. "It's just a bad situation," he said. "You can't help but wonder what would have happened had that door been locked." He also said that the rear door was left unlocked from opening until past closing because employees used it during shift changes and to bring in supplies.

Frank Portillo, president of the 115-restaurant Brown's chain, arrived to extend sympathy to the victims' families. Even though the police had given no official statement, the victims' names were by this time known, thanks to word leaking out to reporters and from other employees participating in the sad process of elimination. Portillo told reporters, his voice choking with emotion, "We all feel this loss personally."

Even though he was no longer connected to the corporation, Fred Brown, whose father had founded the Brown's chain, came to the Palatine police station during the afternoon, offering to help the victims' families. "I feel I owe it to the families and relatives. I do care. It is my name out there," he said. "This is Vietnam all over again. This gets me in my gut. I'm very sorry."

A shocked Palatine mayor Rita Mullins said, "This touches every family that lives within the community."

By early afternoon, clergymen began arriving at the police station and school superintendent Gerald Chapman said that counselors would be available Sunday at Palatine High School, which Castro and Solis had both attended, as did many other Brown's employees.

In the middle of the afternoon, Ken Pittinger, a Brown's employee who had worked the day shift on Friday, was summoned for the grimmest of tasks—identifying the bodies.

It was around 6 P.M. before the last of the seven bodies was removed and people began to drift away. Some of them went home. Others went to church. Some of the teenagers—current and former workers—were at the police station, answering questions. And all of them, in their different ways, were trying desperately to answer a question voiced in the morning by the teenage Georgi: "Who would have thought something like this could happen here? This is a boring town."

THREE

THIS WAS PALATINE AT A GLANCE AT THE END OF 1992:

Population: 42,000

Population change from 1980 to 1991: +23 percent

Racial/ethnic mix: white 90.7 percent; black .9 percent; Hispanic, 3.6 percent; other, 4.8 percent

Area: 10 square miles

Average household income: $58,258

Per capita income: $17,556; 65th of 262 in six-county metropolitan Chicago area

Motto: "A Real Home Town"

The area that would become Palatine was first settled after the 1832 Blackhawk War by New Englanders and

Europeans primarily of German stock who headed for the groves later known as Plum, Highland, Deer, and Englishman's. These cool woodlands that broke the endless prairies were later converted to rich farmland by homesteaders. Palatine itself, the consensus goes, was named for the home of one of its original settlers, Harrison Cook (formerly Koch), a German from Palatine, New York, who apparently maintained the practice of early American settlers, who simply moved the name of their town with them as they traveled westward. Palatine's first town meeting was recorded in 1850, and the village was incorporated in 1866.

Nothing of special historical significance marked Palatine's existence for the remainder of the century. Its main claim to fame then was the high school. Opened in 1875, Palatine High School was the only secondary institution between Jefferson Park on the northwest side of Chicago and the northern Illinois town of Woodstock until the 1920s.

Old Palatine High School, built in 1928 (the original 1875 building was long gone), was converted in 1977 into Cutting Hall, a performing arts center-park district facility adjacent to the village hall and police station. Summer softball games filled the fields by Cutting Hall, while other community activities included the chamber of commerce's "Taste and Touch of Palatine" and the Jaycee-sponsored Fourth of July festivities.

Years ago, residents looked forward to the Cook County Fair, which was held in Palatine, with a half-mile track that featured sulky races and motorcycle races. The town news, as recorded by the newspaper, the *Palatine Enterprise,* symbolized the quiet folksiness of the town:

1909: "Dr. Black's Holsman auto arrived this week. It is the first of the buggy autos owned in town and the result of its action on bad roads will be watched with considerable interest."

1911: "A tribe of Gypsies consisting of 16 wagons camped for several days at Plum Grove until they were requested to move on."

1917: "There are to be no more free lunches in Palatine saloons. Bring your own sandwich and some extra money to pay the increased price of drinks."

1918: "Twenty-five deer will be put in Deer Grove Forest Preserve."

The town was a rural community of two thousand residents until the mid-1940s when returning World War II veterans moved there primarily because housing prices were affordable. Eventually, dairy farms were sold off to make room for subdivisions and the families moving from Chicago. The population grew rapidly from slightly more than four thousand in 1950 to more than twenty-six thousand in 1970. The northwest suburbs were booming with new corporate activity and housing. There was phenomenal population growth in the 1980s, fundamentally changing Palatine from a small town to a small city grappling with problems such as downtown revitalization.

Palatine had niches filled with shops such as Patti's Pretties and Christl's Inn, a German restaurant where you could get a liver and onion plate for $4.45 at lunch. But it also had the sprawling strip developments, where a parade of fast-food emporiums shouldered up to gigantic stores such as Builders Square.

The downtown area was mostly ignored and neglected, as the suburb's growth and expansion was concentrated along Palatine's main arteries: Rand, Dundee, and Palatine Roads, and Northwest Highway. The main downtown drag, Slade Street, was pockmarked with empty stores. Some shoppers lamented the passing of the communal atmosphere of the old downtown, but even they admitted that they liked the abundance of goods available at the larger strip centers. Palatine had no indoor malls where people gather and no central shopping district as such. Business had spidered out along major roads that then blended into neighboring towns without clear distinctions.

No one wanted to walk anymore. They preferred getting into their cars to drive to get something. Some wanted things that didn't belong to them. With the 1980s' population boom, home burglaries inevitably rose in Palatine, from 175 in 1981 to 285 in 1991. Crime came to town as the population doubled and redoubled in the decades of growth. Crime that included drugs and gang activity.

This was a problem common to most every suburb in the United States. The dream was dying—the notion that suburbs would be problem-free places to which city people escape. Cities were indeed plagued by poverty, substance abuse, and crime, but most realized that such troubles did not stop at suburban borders. In that respect, the franchise-choked suburb of Palatine was little different from the communities that surround it—Rolling Meadows, Arlington Heights, and Schaumburg—or those that surrounded most major American cities.

But as far as violent crime was concerned, the murder rate was blissfully low. Here are the yearly statistics for the decade preceding the massacre:

1981: 2

1982: 0

1983: 0

1984: 1

1985: 0

1986: 1

1987: 0

1988: 3

1989: 0

1990: 2

1991: 0

1992: 1

Just a week before the massacre, the local weekly newspaper listed the top ten stories of 1992 in Palatine. In first place was the dispute that resulted in the removal of a Christian symbol from the village seal.

Mayor Rita Mullins came to Palatine in 1958 when the population was eight thousand. "Then, I knew everyone in Palatine, or if I didn't know you, I knew your aunt or your baby-sitter," she recalled a decade after the massacre. "Right up until the murders, there was still a real home-town feeling in Palatine. Everyone trusted everyone. This was perfectly Midwest middle-class America."

That sort of sleepy suburban existence ended the night of January 8, 1993. Whatever innocence still clung to the town was forever lost as Palatine joined a roster of blood-splattered small and suburban towns—one that includes Kilgore, San Ysidro, Holcomb, and Stockton—whose names evoke tragedy too enormous to place in any context.

"The murders not only affected residents, they affected everyone that was ever associated with Palatine," Mullins recalled. "People would say, 'I knew someone who used to live there or work there or my uncle used to pass through here on his way to work.' Everyone had a connection. I was in Washington, D.C., about three weeks after the murders and I happened to walk into an antique store and someone said the actor James Earl Jones was standing nearby. He turned and smiled at me."

She walked over to him and introduced herself. "I'm the mayor of Palatine, Illinois," she said.

Jones took her hand in his and held it, staring directly into her eyes. "I'm so sorry," he said. "I am so sorry."

FOUR

MICHAEL CASTRO LAY IN AN OPEN CASKET. HE wore a red top imprinted with the words U.S. MARINES, a symbol of one of his goals. To the left was an eight-by-ten-inch high-school photograph in which he was wearing a tie and smiling broadly. Inside the casket were embroidered the words: WIND BENEATH MY WINGS.

His mother leaned over to speak to the dead sixteen-year-old. "Michael, you never came home," Epifania Castro said. "When are you coming home? Mike, you're supposed to come back. You just went to work."

As the service neared its end, Michael's older sister, Mary Jane Crow, approached. "When they were about to close the casket . . . I went up to fix Michael's hair," she later recalled. "They'd patched his cheek where one of the bullets had gone in, and as I went to fix his hair, I felt the back of his head. And it was gone."

Down the hall in the Ahlgrim & Sons Funeral Home in Palatine, the family of seventeen-year-old Rico Solis was gathering. Flowers from local hospitals, Palatine High School, friends, and sympathetic strangers lined the hallway. It was Tuesday, three days after the massacre.

Many of the boys' friends were not as tearful as they had expected to be. Some of the emotions had been spent at school on Monday, which began with a moment of silence, which followed these words from principal Nancy Robb over the school's public-address system to the nineteen hundred students: "We feel most intimately the loss of two members of our school family."

"Not many people talked because they're still in shock," Jackie Gamroth, a senior, told the *Chicago Tribune*. "The question of 'Why?' just kept coming up."

In some classes, that brief moment of silence lasted as long as fifteen minutes. "No one really knew what to say," said Dan McCloskey, a junior.

More than a hundred students, too emotional to concentrate, left classes and sought counseling from social workers, psychologists, and teachers. "We just wanted to let out what we felt—shock," said Cassandra Fier, who, along with her friend Missy Werner, spent second period with a counselor. "They were so young."

As the school bells rang to begin and end periods, the talk in the hallways, in classrooms, and over lunch focused on trying to cope with the tragedy. "Students are trying to make sense out of a totally irrational situation," said counselor Marc Denny.

Reporters wandered the halls with notebooks, recording the moments as, overcome with emotion, friends of the two teenage victims broke down in tears during classes and in the middle of the school's wide, carpeted hallways.

Most of the students who showed up the next day at the funeral home wore light blue ribbons, in memory of the victims, on their jackets and lapels. They had been distributed at the school, which also gathered $1,500 in a quickly organized fund-raiser to help pay funeral expenses for the two teenagers. "Even if you don't know the people, they're still like family if they go to high school with you," said senior Josh Glorch.

What those who weren't friends of the boys didn't know was that Castro enjoyed music, dancing, and driving his pickup. Classmates had nicknamed him "M.C.," after the dancer and rap star Hammer, formerly known as M. C. Hammer. They didn't know that when he witnessed his first snowfall a couple of months before, Solis was so excited that he celebrated by having a snowball fight with his two sisters for more than an hour.

Some of them might not have known that Castro and Solis were close friends.

Solis was the only son and the eldest of three children. In 1987, his father, Ramon, was stabbed to death in the Philippines. He and his two younger sisters, Jade and Jizelle, came to the United States in May 1992 to live with their mother, Evelyn, who had married again, to Adriano Urgena, and had been living in the United States since 1987.

One of the first people Rico met was Castro, the youngest of four children and a second-generation Filipino. They became quick friends. Castro shepherded Solis through the tribulations of high school, and helped him polish his English.

The boys played video games together, shared an interest in cars, dressed alike, and even mimicked each other's speech. Both took great pride in their vehicles.

Solis drove a 1984 red Dodge Charger, which he bought from his stepfather. He was saving money to buy a sportier car. Castro, who played with radio-controlled cars, drove a white Nissan pickup truck, which he had spruced up.

In October, Şolis took a job at Brown's, where Castro was already working. "They really liked each other; they were always laughing and talking," said Celso Morales, a Brown's employee who worked with the two boys. "When Mike was working, Rico was much happier. He felt more comfortable. When Mike wasn't there, he talked, but he wouldn't laugh like he was having fun. They were both so much alike."

More so than many thought. On the Sunday morning following the massacre, the families of the boys had gathered at the funeral home, and while consoling one another, they realized that Michael's uncle and Rico's grandfather shared the same last name, Laureano, and both were natives of the same province in the Philippines. Realizing that the dead boys were likely cousins, the families held their wakes at the same time and place.

"It was very emotional for us to find out, a very big coincidence," Consuelo Santos, Solis's aunt, said of the possible blood link between the boys.

Death has a way of joining lives together in mysterious ways. As Eugene Kennedy pointed out in his essay in the *Tribune* days after the massacre, "There, on that shadowed night they stood together, much like the characters in Thornton Wilder's famous novel, 'The Bridge of San Luis Rey.' Strangers to each other, they had made their way by very different paths to that still point of mystery to which, all unknowing, they had been hurrying together. As they were crossing, the bridge collapsed, and if the public cause was the fraying rope, the secret cause lay in the fullness of their lives. That mystery, of how we all stand at the edge of the bridge of destiny, the seemingly tangled purposes of our lives cast before us as surely as a fisherman's line, will remain even after the other mysteries of Palatine are solved."

Many of the two hundred people who gathered for a Catholic memorial service for Guadalupe Maldonado at Santa Teresita Church in Palatine did not speak English. The ceremony, conducted in Spanish and English, began at 7 P.M. in the church's dimly lit sanctuary, while Spanish hymns played quietly in the background.

"He was kind and quiet," Sister Rosita Maria said of Maldonado. "But he always, whenever he could, helped around the church, clearing the snow and things like that."

Services for Marcus Nellsen took place in the Montclair-Lucania Funeral Home on the northwest side of Chicago. Nellsen had begun working at Brown's in November, and had shown great ambition, aspiring to become a manager for the fast-food chain. A nine-year veteran of the U.S. Navy, Nellsen had also worked at a manufacturing plant before being laid off when the plant closed in August 1992.

"He would always brag about how he was going to go to Brown's Chicken school to learn to be an assistant manager," said Celso Morales.

A friend said that Nellsen's past had been marked by troubles, including a difficult divorce and unspecified hardships in finding his place in life. "He was a fellow struggling with life's problems," said Randy Fischer, a resident of the Lincoln-Belmont YMCA on Chicago's north side, where Nellsen had recently lived. "Given the fact that he was not well equipped to handle them, I thought he was doing an excellent job."

Fischer said Nellsen had moved out of the YMCA several months earlier after living there for a year and a half. He had moved in with his girlfriend, Joy McClain, in Palatine, within walking distance of the restaurant. They were planning on getting married. The thirty-one-year-old Nellsen, according to Morales, "used to brag about his fifty-one-year-old girlfriend" and talk about "this fitness bike that he used to ride an hour a day. We would always tell him that was too much because he smoked a lot."

Services were held for Thomas Mennes at the Ahlgrim & Sons Funeral Home. A lifelong resident of Palatine and a bachelor, Mennes had never finished high school. He often could be seen riding his bicycle around town to a variety of jobs that seemed to change with the seasons. He had worked at a Popeye's chicken restaurant in Palatine, at a Piggly Wiggly grocery store, and at a roofing company before taking the job at Brown's. Friends, coworkers, and relatives described him as a loner who liked to watch TV and who bowled on Tuesday nights. Mennes lived with his twin brother, Jerry, who said that Thomas was an "easygoing guy. He had a girlfriend, but he was not the type to get married. He liked to hang out in the forest preserves and liked the rock groups Rush, Pink Floyd, and Led Zeppelin."

"He tried to do the best he could in life. He was not a talkative boy," said his stepmother, Francis Mennes. She was married to Thomas's father, Emil, who was partially paralyzed as the result of a stroke and had previously lost another son, John, who died in 1989 of a heart attack. "Thomas was such a loner, it's hard to know much about him," said a neighbor who lived on the same block.

In contrast, so much was known about Richard and Lynn Ehlenfeldt.

Richard was born and grew up in Columbus, a town of four thousand about twenty-five miles northeast of Madison, Wisconsin. His father ran the Eager Beaver laundry service there and was once mayor. Richard had studied for the Methodist ministry and later held jobs in Democratic politics, serving as an aide to Wisconsin governor Martin Schreiber and working in the presidential campaigns of Robert Kennedy, Hubert Humphrey, George McGovern, and Jimmy Carter. He also served as an assistant secretary of state in Wisconsin.

Lynn Ehlenfeldt grew up in Waupaca, about a hundred miles north of Columbus. After she married Richard, the couple lived in Madison. She was a dedicated mother who devoted herself to social causes such as hunger and homelessness. Before that, she had worked as an advocate for the mentally retarded and directed a halfway house for abused women. She had also been a soccer coach for her children.

"They were two of the most caring people I ever knew," friend and former Wisconsin secretary of state Doug La Follette said in a statement to the media.

In 1989, Richard had been laid off from Group W Cable after it was purchased by Prime Cable, of Austin, Texas. He had been a vice president and a director of government and public affairs.

The Ehlenfeldts had been married for twenty-five years and had three daughters, Joy, Dana, and Jennifer. All three graduated from Buffalo Grove High School and were active in soccer.

After Joy, the youngest, graduated from high school in the spring of 1992, Richard and Lynn bought the Brown's restaurant, pouring most of their assets, and most of their time, into the chicken franchise. They worked long hours in the restaurant, putting in double shifts to learn their new trade.

They were part of a growing crowd. "Recession has given a surprising shot in the arm to the growth of franchise ownership," wrote the *Tribune*'s Andrew Leckey that year. "Increasing executive layoffs mean a greater number of highly qualified Americans are considering franchises. Displaced workers often receive a cash payoff when they leave their original firm, and they are likely to have built up equity in their home, which they can borrow against to get started. As a result, the franchise industry is growing at a 6 to 10 percent annual clip."

But, Leckey warned, "Not all franchises are a sure thing."

Before the couple bought the franchise, they had earned a reputation as active members of their community. Richard was president of the homeowners' association in the affluent Arlington Heights subdivision where the family had lived since 1985. Lynn volunteered for community organizations and was active with school issues. A next-door neighbor, Colette Urban, said Lynn brought brownies to welcome her to the neighborhood when she moved there in 1989. "That's the way they were," Urban said. "They were very friendly, outgoing people."

But after they bought the restaurant, neighbor Robert Becker said, "We never saw them, Dick said it was a lot of long hours, but that is what it took to succeed."

Services for the Ehlenfeldts were held at the church where they had volunteered so many hours—Kingswood Methodist Church in Buffalo Grove, just to the west of

Palatine. They were buried in Memorial Gardens Cemetery in Arlington Heights.

Castro and Solis were buried in All Saints Cemetery in Des Plaines, as was Mennes. Nellsen was buried in Memory Gardens Cemetery in Arlington Heights. Maldonado's body was returned to Mexico for burial.

Friends and relatives paid their respects in various ways. Perhaps none was more poignant or symbolic than what Teri McMillan, a friend of the Ehlenfeldts, did that day. After services for the couple, she drove alone to Brown's. It was raining, a cold hard rain. Slowly McMillan walked from her car. The parking lot, or a portion of it, was still encircled by the yellow police tape. She saw no police officers. She stood for a few minutes staring at the building. She leaned down and laid a bouquet of carnations on a mound of crusted snow.

They were white, pink, and red. There were seven of them.

FIVE

___

IN THE IMMEDIATE MOMENTS AFTER A CRIME IS discovered, crime scene technicians—the techs, as they are often called—are among the most important personnel to be summoned. And, as any veteran watcher of television crime shows is aware, the integrity of the scene must be protected from anyone who might, even unwittingly, disturb or destroy possible evidence. It is during these first few hours that a case can be made or lost. And time is essential.

Within minutes of the discovery of the dead bodies at Brown's, calls went out requesting crime scene investigators from the Cook County sheriff's police as well as from the Northern Illinois Police Crime Lab. They were on the premises by 4 A.M.

The Northern Illinois Police Crime Lab had begun operating in 1968 in offices within the headquarters of the Highland Park Police Department on the shore of Lake Michigan, north of Chicago. Until then, suburban police

departments had submitted their lab work to the Chicago
Police Department, but as the crime rate and particularly
the need for processing of seized narcotics increased dramatically, the Chicago police lab developed a chronic
backlog and ultimately discontinued services to munici-
palities outside of Cook County.

The lab was the realization of a dream of Michael Bonamarte II, a former Highland Park police chief and a
thirty-eight-year veteran of law enforcement. In 1968,
Bonamarte and Andrew H. Principe, a former Chicago
Police Department chemist, founded the lab as a nonprofit
corporation to serve suburban law enforcement agencies.

So, seven suburbs whose police departments individu-
ally did not have the manpower, money, or expertise to
have their own forensic laboratory banded together to un-
derwrite the new laboratory. By the time of the Palatine
murders, the lab was staffed with ten forensic analysts
who worked on behalf of forty-six different police agencies and conducted tests on five thousand to six thousand
cases annually.

The lab was divided into several sections. In the fingerprint section, examiners compared fingerprints from
crime scenes to prints on file with the Illinois State Police
database. In the firearms section, analysts examined guns,
test-fired them, and compared markings on the bullet or
casing to bullets and casings in the open-case file, which
housed unsolved cases from all member communities. The
biology department dealt with DNA testing. The trace department dealt with such crimes as arson, in which case
the lab examined evidence for traces of accelerants.

When technicians arrived at the Palatine murder scene,
they found a perimeter set up to control access to the
parking lot immediately outside the restaurant. The name

of every person who entered the area was recorded on a sign-in sheet.

The restaurant itself was also secured, and technicians processed the scene a section at a time. No police detectives were allowed inside any of the sections until the evidence gathering had been completed. Every person who went inside was required to don plastic foot protectors and gloves to prevent the creation of false footprints or fingerprints.

Painstakingly, the technicians dusted for prints, took swabs of blood, and working on their hands and knees, pored over every inch of the restaurant.

As the technicians were meticulously going about their tasks, Jane Homeyer, a forensic scientist from the northern Illinois lab with a doctorate in chemistry, donned a pair of gloves and began to scour the room. Homeyer had just turned twenty-nine three days earlier. She was widely regarded by those in the field as a top analyst. She had begun her career working on forgeries and handwriting analysis and would eventually become executive director of the Highland Park–based crime lab, and later, director of the forensic training unit at the FBI Academy in Quantico, Virginia.

Homeyer, a slender woman with sandy brown hair and wire-rim eyeglasses, had the appearance of a lawyer. "Jane looked like a prosecutor straight out of law school," a fellow analyst later recalled. "She was fastidious and meticulous—traits that she carried over to her work as a scientist." As other technicians were dusting for fingerprints, taking measurements of blood spots, and photographing the bodies, Homeyer began opening the garbage containers in the customer area of the restaurant.

"What the hell are you doing?" another technician asked.

"Looking for evidence," she replied in a calm and even voice. "I'm looking for evidence."

As she opened the bins, she noticed that the containers were empty and the plastic liners were clean. She suspected strongly that the bins had been emptied as part of the day's-end cleanup. She opened another bin and peered inside. There, at the bottom of the plastic liner bag, was the detritus—bones and gristle—of a chicken meal. Was it the last meal prepared in the restaurant that day? Could it have been a meal ordered by the killer?

Carefully, Homeyer removed the entire liner bag and rebagged it as a precaution, even though she could not be sure the residue of the meal would be of any evidentiary value. Homeyer could not know if the food might lead to identifying a suspect in the massacre, but she followed her training to gather any and all possible evidence.

As a forensic analyst, she was aware that bite-mark technology had been used to solve crimes in the past. As a scientist, she was particularly aware that the emerging technology of DNA testing could come into play. Yet Homeyer also was aware that DNA testing used in criminal prosecutions was largely limited to blood and semen. There was no way of knowing if those materials were on the chicken and the likelihood seemed remote. At the same time Homeyer knew that the science of DNA testing was evolving almost monthly and perhaps, she thought, the testing procedures would improve enough that if any such evidence was left on the chicken bones, it could be identified. Later that day, the bag of partially eaten chicken and bones was put into a freezer at the Palatine Police Department.

Federal Bureau of Investigation technicians were also on the scene, processing fingerprints and gathering evidence using fluorescent powders, a technique that was, at the time, on the cutting edge of forensic science. Later, bullets removed from the victims would be sent to the Chicago Police Crime Lab for analysis in case a weapon was recovered and ballistics comparisons could be made. At the Chicago lab, the bullets would be compared to dozens of guns seized during street arrests in the hope that the murder weapon would be found. Processing the scene took seven days. Analyzing the evidence would take weeks, even months.

"In this case," Chief Bratcher told the media a month after the massacre, "I doubt there has been a more thorough crime scene search on any case that has ever come down the pike. We have a large volume of evidence still being processed. This is an asset we have." He reported that the technicians had retrieved scores of fingerprints, as well as blood, hair, fiber, and bullets from the kitchen of the restaurant. Hundreds of pages of business records were recovered as well, as the investigators had hauled out dozens of yellow evidence bags containing potential evidence.

Bratcher also said police would use a new $2 million Automatic Fingerprint Identification System, a computer program that transforms fingerprints to mathematical equations that can be quickly compared to other fingerprints stored in the system's database. The system, he said, can compare even the smallest of fragments of prints with the more than one million prints in the database.

Ultimately, a separate computer database would be constructed and every piece of information—tips, leads, and evidence—would be logged in the hope that somehow, something would match or fall into place that the investigators had overlooked.

Investigators subsequently assigned to work on the Brown's massacre first had to endure a ghastly initiation. Each was made to view a detailed videotape of the crime scene, one recorded by police in the dark hours after the slaughter. Those who watched this tape, even veteran detectives, would later describe its contents with a single word: vicious.

As more information began to surface about the killings, it appeared that the victims likely endured a horror-filled encounter. New details released by investigators in the week following the crime suggested the killer came to commit a robbery, but, frustrated when it did not go smoothly, may have tortured some of the victims before executing the married owners of the restaurant along with their five employees.

Investigators constructed a likely series of events after the restaurant's 9 P.M. closing.

They suspected that more than one person entered the restaurant, rounded up workers, and demanded money, threatening violence before slashing Lynn Ehlenfeldt's throat.

It was then that the shooting began. The sequence in which the victims were killed was unclear to investigators, but the wounds sustained by the two youngest workers, Castro and Solis, indicated that the two may have tried to interrupt the robbery by resisting the gunmen.

Richard Ehlenfeldt and the cook, Marcus Nellsen, were found on the floor in the walk-in cooler near the back of the restaurant while the other five victims were found on top of one another in the walk-in freezer, probably collapsing as they were shot after being herded inside.

The entire episode probably took about forty minutes, a time estimate based on the discovery of the wall clock that was stopped at 9:50. Investigators didn't know why the clock stopped, but surmised there had been some sort of power failure or that a ricochet from one of the bullets somehow damaged the clock.

Police believed the killers entered the restaurant about ten minutes past closing, after the last customers had walked out. The bloody mop found in the restaurant might have been used to clean the scene or may have been simply stained in the aftermath of the killings.

Almost immediately, some residents questioned whether Palatine police were experienced enough to handle this investigation, given the history of the department. Police protection in the village of Palatine began soon after being approved at a meeting on April 10, 1866. Among the duties of the first constable was building a pound for housing horses, sheep, pigs, and dogs and serving as the pound master. The constable also enforced the laws and ordinances of the time, such as "no butchering within 140 rods center of said corporate town of Palatine."

The constable also had to collect license fees from "peddlers and showmen" and make sure all saloonkeepers closed their doors at 11 P.M. He received no salary but was compensated with twenty-five cents for each license fee he collected and from fines levied against saloons that stayed open past their appointed closing hour. The constable carried a gun that was used exclusively to kill dogs running at large. He was in charge of burying them, and for that he was paid fifty cents per dog.

The first true cops in the village were hired in the 1870s and paid one dollar per night as "night policemen." By 1890, there was a "special policeman" making $425 a year for performing duties that included acting as night watchman, lamplighter, and taking care of the fire engine.

The first uniformed officers were on the job in 1913, but the first salaried chief of police, a fellow named Charles G. Folz, was not appointed until February 9, 1942. He oversaw two policemen, and the "force" grew to four men in 1946 and to five by 1949. The next year, Herbert Moehling was appointed chief, and by the time Harold Nehmzow took over the department at the new Village Hall, there were ten policemen including the chief, three radio operators, and a secretary. They worked three shifts, six days a week, each shift with two patrolmen and a sergeant. They often worked overtime on Sundays in the 1960s as a result of heavy traffic returning from the many popular weekend vacation spots in Wisconsin to the north.

In March 1973, Chief Robert Center was demoted to lieutenant and Frank Ortiz, the department's first detective, was named to serve as the interim acting chief until the end of that year. That's when Jerry Bratcher came on board.

He found a police department in which morale was low. Center had resigned following charges filed by the Palatine Board of Fire and Police Commissioners accusing him of failure to perform internal administrative duties and failure to enforce laws against overweight trucks in the village.

A former sergeant in the U.S. Marines, Bratcher had first worked as a cop at the DeKalb, Illinois, force, rising from patrol officer in 1956 to commander of patrol, traffic, and detective divisions by 1963. He left the department in 1965 for the Regency Life Insurance Co., where in four years he became director of sales.

But the lure of police work brought him back in 1969 when he was named chief of the department in Rochelle, an Illinois city of ten thousand near DeKalb, to clean up a mess. The city's force was the target of widespread charges of police corruption and ineptitude. In four years, he turned the department around so successfully that the Illinois Chamber of Commerce described its force as "one of the most effective and professional police agencies" in the state. Bratcher would later say that his work in Rochelle was a "unique opportunity to become the change agent instrumental in transforming a police department from a symbol of community embarrassment to one of pride."

He was selected as Palatine chief following a national search and his first task was to reorganize and professionalize a department he found to be "backward" and "improperly managed." His department was one of the first in the state to be accredited by the Commission on Accreditation for Law Enforcement Agencies, the first department in the state to have a local crime prevention unit, and the first to have a drug awareness unit. He also created a multiagency major crime task force.

During his first twelve years at Palatine, he also found time to attend college, where he obtained a bachelor of arts degree, a master's degree in public administration, and a master's degree in law enforcement administration.

In charge of a staff of sixty, Bratcher instantly stamped himself a progressive by embracing the newest crime-fighting techniques while working within the constraints of a small-town police department budget.

Still, even before the Brown's Chicken victims were buried, the department was subjected to serious second-guessing. Only three days after the bodies were discov-

ered, one newspaper went so far as to suggest that the
investigation appeared to be "foundering." The charge
was prompted by the way investigators had handled an
anonymous telephone tip that came in on January 9 at
11:38 A.M., while the bodies were still being examined
inside the restaurant.

The caller was a woman. She mentioned the name of
twenty-three-year-old Martin Blake, who had been recently fired from the restaurant. She said that he owned a
gun that he had been using for target practice. The police
soon discovered that Blake had a record: he had been
arrested three years earlier for the theft of a radar detector
and just the summer before on a charge of reckless driving.

A further check of Brown's employment records
showed that Blake had been a cook at the restaurant until
a week before the killings, when he was fired by owner
Richard Ehlenfeldt. He had also previously dated Michael
Castro's older sister, Mary Jane. Finally, and most encouraging to police, Blake fit a description provided by a
passerby who said he saw a man hanging around the back
of the restaurant on the night of the massacre.

Not long after the anonymous call, police disguised as
utility workers in Commonwealth Edison and Northern
Illinois Gas trucks and uniforms began arriving outside of
Blake's two-story home in the suburb of Elgin. At 2:56
P.M., Blake emerged, walked to his 1977 Ford Bronco,
and lifted the hood.

Immediately fifteen officers rushed him, guns drawn,
and took him into custody. Other officers entered the
house and conducted a search, removing plumbing and
tearing insulation from the walls. Two large plastic bags
of material were removed.

For two days, Blake was interrogated, but investigators

made no headway. He offered an alibi: he had been drinking with friends at his home and had left just once to buy more beer. He took a polygraph exam and passed. Blake's gun was a .22-caliber pistol. The victims had been shot with .38-caliber bullets.

On January 11, after attorneys for Blake insisted that police charge their client or release him, Palatine police let him go.

Cook County state's attorney Jack O'Malley said that while "no one has been eliminated as a suspect," Blake had been cut loose unconditionally. With no quick solution apparent, critics pounced, demanding to know why the police had taken so long to discover the crime: the bodies were not found until nearly six hours after the restaurant closed. They brought up the disturbing fact that the initial checks of the restaurant were so perfunctory that police missed discovering that one of its doors was unlocked.

The most vocal critic was Emmanuel Castro, Michael Castro's father, a businessman himself who operated a variety store on Chicago's northwest side that sold, among many items, guns. His criticism was bolstered by outsiders, such as Steve Egger, chairman of the criminal justice program at Sangamon State University in Springfield, Illinois. He told the *Chicago Sun-Times* that it was "certainly a possibility" that the ethnic backgrounds of the Maldonado and Castro families played a role in the response of police to their concerns. Castro, a Filipino immigrant, said he thought his complaints were not taken seriously "because of our accent, because of our look."

The delay in the discovery of the bodies, some argued, might have been disastrous. Family members were haunted by the possibility that one of the victims might have still been alive at the time of the first visit by police. Some theorized, that not only might lives have been saved, but perhaps some vital clues—even a description of the killers—had been lost forever as a result.

"If someone was still living, gasping for breath, we might have saved his life," Emmanuel Castro said.

There is little doubt that during the two-day investigation of Blake, all tips and other leads were put on hold. Though investigators did interview a number of workers and residents of the neighborhood surrounding the restaurant on the day after the murders, an exhaustive canvassing of the area took weeks to complete.

Other critics cried foul when they discovered that Bratcher had waited three days before calling in the FBI, which dispatched a team led by Jim Bell from the agency's Investigative Support Unit, a division that handles serial crimes. Bell and his unit had been involved in investigating two of the nation's most notorious serial killing cases: the Green River murders in the state of Washington and coed killer Ted Bundy.

After he was convicted of the 1978 rape and murder of a twelve-year-old Florida girl, Bundy had admitted his string of murders in Washington, Utah, Florida, and Colorado during a conversation with an agent assigned to Bell's unit. Bundy, of Tacoma, confessed to more than twenty murders before he was executed in Florida's electric chair in 1989, although authorities believe that he actually killed closer to forty women. Ironically, Bundy's admissions came when he was attempting to help the unit solve the Green River murders: a still unsolved case in which forty-nine women disappeared or were killed in the Seattle area from 1982 through 1984. The Green River killer was prolific, slaying up to five women in a month.

It remains the largest serial murder case in the country. Fifty-two-year-old Gary Leon Ridgway was arrested in 2001 and charged with aggravated first-degree murder in the deaths of seven of the women whose deaths were blamed on the Green River killer.

In Palatine, Bell and the unit went about their business as they always did: comparing information from a crime scene against the wealth of FBI data obtained from thousands of interviews with killers, and then coming up with a composite. They attempt to categorize a murder scene as the work of an organized killer (one that is well planned and left few clues) or a disorganized killer (one that appears to be a spur-of-the-moment crime). The unit studies photographs from the crime scene, autopsy photos and results, police reports, and a wide assortment of evidentiary and investigative materials.

But in Palatine, Bell and his unit were unable to create a profile of the killer because of the possibility that more than one person was involved, though they did develop and share theories on how and why the crime was committed by studying the scene. The Palatine Police Department had to keep that information under wraps, however, even as it continued to suffer increasing criticism. Indeed, the force felt so assailed that on the morning of January 15, Deputy Chief Walter Gasior began what had become his regular morning news briefing by handing out a sheaf of positive comments about the police investigators that had been obtained from businesspeople and local citizens.

That defensive posture was primarily prompted, many believed, by the editorial that morning in the *Chicago Tribune* that sharply criticized the department. "It is becoming worrisomely apparent that Palatine police may be as baffled about basic investigative procedure as they are about whodunit," the newspaper stated. "Though it may not affect the outcome, it may have cost the police a valuable edge early on and it clearly undermines confidence in the department's ability to lead the case . . . it is now undisputed that police failed to treat seriously information from several family members of citizens, alarmed that their relatives hadn't come home the night of the crime.

"Equally troubling now is their performance in the aftermath, when they realized they were dealing with a massive crime," the editorial continued, focusing on what it considered the delay in the canvassing of witnesses. "Law enforcement experts point out that this kind of door-to-door spadework is textbook police procedure. It also is obvious to anyone who has ever seen a TV cop show. Failure to move quickly risks leads turning cold, suspects getting farther away and people forgetting what may turn out to be important details."

The investigation took what some called, even in the face of such a grimly serious matter, an almost comical turn that afternoon. It began about 2 P.M. when two tipsters telephoned the special hotline set up by police to report they had overheard four men from a suburb near Palatine admit that they were involved in the murders.

A promising lead? Perhaps, but by then the department had already logged more than a thousand telephone calls since the discovery of the bodies. And many of those calls, while coming from well-meaning citizens, were proving worthless.

When investigators were slow to follow up on the call alerting them to the overheard conversation, the tipsters called local ABC news reporter Chuck Goudie, an award-winning investigator for station WLS, Channel 7. He agreed to meet with them later that day.

Goudie was with them when Palatine investigators finally telephoned to follow up the lead. He listened as the tipsters recounted their information. As authorities would later recall, the overheard conversation of the four men contained information that was at sharp odds with the facts that police knew about the killings. Still, authorities decided the four individuals were worth interviewing, if for no other reason than that one had an outstanding warrant for the robbery of a clothing store a year earlier.

Goudie and a WLS camera crew staked out the apartment where the four men lived, waiting for Palatine police to descend on it as they had descended upon Martin Blake just days earlier. But the police did not come that night. The following day, Goudie told investigators that he was going to go on the air and report the story told by the informants. He could tell it one of two ways: the four were in custody, or police were ignoring the lead.

Though they would later say that they were not reacting to the ultimatum, it didn't take long for the police to act. They arrived at the apartment and took away six people, three men and three women. In contrast to the way Blake had been arrested, the six were casually led to waiting police cars.

Goudie had his story, and on the news there he was, saying that six people were taken into custody, that one of the men had confessed to the killings, and that police were seeking a seventh person. As columnist Eric Zorn wrote in the *Tribune:* "Police came to Schaumburg and took away three of the four implicated men early in the afternoon, and Channel 7 was there to record the obviously nonchalant loading of the men into cars, and to follow them with cameras back to Palatine. The men were named and all but tried and convicted on the airwaves before investigation spokesmen had said a word. Goudie and the Channel 7 news team laid out the entire massacre scenario, named the gunman, described the motive and indicated that at least one of the men had confessed."

It appeared to be a major break in the case. But within three hours, police announced that all the suspects were being released except the one man who was being held on warrants for the suburban robbery on December 29 and for failure to appear on an aggravated assault charge.

Yet again a promising lead had gone nowhere and the word *unsolved* began to hang heavier than ever on the Palatine Police Department. At the same time, some knowledgeable law enforcement officials remained confident; they knew that when it came to solving crimes, Chief Bratcher was patient and tenacious. He had proven this once before and he would, they felt, prove it again.

Three years after he became chief, Bratcher had been charged with investigating the disappearance of Stephanie Anne Lyng, who vanished without a trace on October 27, 1977. Police said the thirty-nine-year-old homemaker and daughter of Chicago newspaper columnist Dorsey Connors had left her Palatine home about 9 A.M. They said she drove five blocks to the home of a friend, the mother of a Girl Scout, to drop off a check to pay for a scouting trip for one of her daughters. The friend said Lyng told her she had to return home because workers were to arrive to lay carpeting. The workers said their knocks at the Lyngs' front door went unanswered. Three days later, the car Stephanie owned with her husband, Edward, a blue station wagon, turned up abandoned at O'Hare International Airport. It was stained with blood.

Over the years, police interviewed dozens of people, followed up hundreds of tips and leads, and conducted at least two digs at rural sites, hoping to find a sign of the missing woman. Nothing materialized.

Then, nearly twenty years later, came a break. Police were investigating—ironically, at Edward Lyng's insistence—the charge that seven people were stealing money from the vending routes that he controlled as owner of Lyng's vending company. One of those whom the police interviewed was James Schweiger. During the questioning, Schwieger implicated Lyng and his girlfriend, Rezba Knutson, in the disappearance of Lyng's wife.

Police then interviewed Knutson, who said that on the morning Stephanie Lyng disappeared, Edward Lyng called her to say that he needed a ride back from O'Hare. She said Lyng created an alibi for the trip and, within a month of the disappearance, revealed to her details of what he allegedly said was his wife's slaying.

Knutson, who was not charged with any crime in exchange for her cooperation, later gave this account of the murder in court: Lyng told her he left the couple's home early that morning only to return, park his car a short distance away, and enter the house. There he waited for his wife in the family room. After she returned from dropping off the Girl Scout check, he struck her on the head with a gun, tied her up, and stabbed her with a knife. Knutson said Lyng told her he wrapped up his wife's body, cleaned up the blood, and drove the body in the couple's station wagon to a site in Lake County. There, he buried her.

As a result of these interviews, the investigation of the case was revived in October 1992, and a grand jury returned an indictment charging the fifty-eight-year-old Edward Lyng with murder. As a motive, investigators cited Lyng's marital problems and that he did not want to share his assets if the couple divorced. State's attorney O'Malley said Lyng was arrested at O'Hare as he was about to fly to Egypt. He added that the absence of a body was not a legal obstacle to prosecuting Lyng—and a jury confirmed that with a guilty verdict in 1994.

"I am so relieved," Stephanie's mother, Dorsey Connors, said afterward. "Dear God, I think prayers do help. The [Palatine] police and state's attorney's office have done a remarkable job. I am a Democrat, but let me tell you that office is running like a well-oiled machine."

O'Malley, a Republican just elected to a second term, also congratulated Palatine police, noting how closely and efficiently Chief Bratcher had worked with prosecutors. "Police investigators under Bratcher and top aides Jack McGregor and Kenneth Mrozek never let up," O'Malley said.

Bratcher had been tight-lipped throughout the Lyng case as he would later be following the Brown's massacre. He told the media that police had developed information about the manner of Stephanie Lyng's death, but he said he would not talk about it until trial. "We have always been ready to investigate any lead over the years," Bratcher said. "This case was never closed."

SIX

THREE DAYS AFTER THE MASSACRE, A TASK FORCE was formally organized. investigators from the Chicago Police Department, the Cook County Sheriff's Police, the FBI, the Illinois State Police, and departments in several surrounding suburbs were dispatched. These investigators were veterans of scores of murder cases and brought with them a vast collection of skills—in the art of interrogation, following leads, tracking down suspects, and analyzing clues.

Within days, their sheer number prompted the task force to move out of the Palatine Police Department and into space in a vacant Palatine school building. Photographs of the victims were taped to the walls, which quickly filled up with maps, diagrams, and bulletins. Clipboards containing "lead sheets" hung from nails hammered into the walls. Computers were hauled in and set up to begin the arduous task of typing in all the reports that were quickly accumulating. Two thirty-cup coffee urns were filled and drained at least four times a day. Roll calls were held twice and three times a day so that information could be passed from one team of investigators to another, keeping the task force members uniformly informed about developments.

At first there were two shifts of twelve hours each, but many investigators worked even longer and some had to be ordered to go home to sleep. About once a week, someone would be sent to the Vienna Sausage factory in Chicago to pick up five or ten pounds of hot dogs, which were cooked on a grill that was set up on a patio outside a rear door. Some men wouldn't even take time to go out for lunch. This was not the doughnut crowd of cops. "These guys were so into this case I couldn't believe it," Chicago homicide sergeant Paul Carroll, who was assigned to the task force at the beginning, later recalled. "We wanted to solve this case so badly. The photos of the crime were sickening. We wanted to solve it for the families."

Among the hundreds of tips that flooded the task force were telephone calls from suburban police departments to report recent armed robberies that bore similarities to the Brown's murders. Although none of the victims in these robberies had been injured, in some of the cases workers were herded into walk-in coolers and freezers before the robbers fled. "This is one of the strongest investigative avenues we are pursing at this point," Palatine Deputy Police Chief Gasior said less than a week after the massacre.

Some of these other robberies bore little resemblance to the Brown's case, except that the establishments that were robbed were in the business of selling food. Yet investigators, struggling to find leads, any sort of leads, pored over the reports so thoroughly that they were able to find nuggets that were at least momentarily tantalizing.

In north suburban Mundelein, the Super Mexico grocery store had been held up on December 7, 1992, by five men who entered the store about 9 P.M., pretending to be customers. After a few moments, two of the men drew weapons, one a handgun and the other a knife, and ordered three employees into a cooler. The robbers fled with $2,000.

A Taco Bell in the nearby suburb of Des Plaines had been held up on December 19, just three weeks before the Palatine murders, by three masked gunmen who forced the three workers into the cooler. Police said about an hour after the restaurant closed at 2 A.M., an employee had walked outside and was confronted by the gunmen. A manager opened a floor safe for the robbers, who then ordered the employees into the cooler. The employees were told to remain there for fifteen minutes while the robbers escaped.

On December 22, Castillo's Groceries in the nearby suburb of Arlington Heights was robbed. There, too, workers had been forced into a cooler. But police there downplayed any connection to the Brown's murders. "This is not connected to Palatine," said Arlington Heights police lieutenant Michael Ossler. "That is where they are going right now, but we're not saying there is a big connection." He noted that no violence had occurred.

And on December 29, a bakery worker in Skokie, another nearby suburb, had been held up and robbed of his paycheck by a gunman who put a pistol to his head.

Two men were already in custody on charges of participating in some of these robberies, but both were believed to have been part of a gang of six or seven people who would split up into pairs to do their heists.

Though task force investigators were understandably concentrating their efforts in the suburbs, they were also intrigued by holdups in Chicago.

One such robbery occurred on December 6 at a Captain Video Store on the city's northwest side. Two men, one armed with a blue steel semiautomatic, forced employees into a storage room and escaped with about $500. And just three days before the Brown's massacre, two men robbed the Wolfhound Pub in the same neighborhood. One of those robbers, also armed with a blue steel semiautomatic pistol, ordered the owner to open the restaurant safe while the other robber took money from another employee.

Of further interest was what took place at about 8:30 P.M. on January 12, when two masked men entered a Little Caesar's pizzeria in Crown Point, Indiana, about seventy miles southeast of Palatine. One carried a sawed-off shotgun, the other a knife. They leaped over the counter and forced three workers, two of whom were teenagers, into a walk-in cooler. The robbers wedged a dish rack against the cooler door and escaped. No one was harmed.

Soon a pattern appeared to the more optimistic investigators, who thought—or hoped—that there was a link to a rash of robberies along a swath of south suburban Chicago and northwest Indiana in the two months before the Palatine murders. Robbers had hit another Taco Bell, this one in Alsip, and robbed a Little Caesar's pizzeria and Rigetta's pizza parlor in Lansing, a Clark gas station in Blue Island, a carryout restaurant in South Holland, and an Arby's in Munster, Indiana.

But as the investigators pressed further, the leads weakened and fizzled out completely. Two of three men named as suspects in some of the unsolved robberies in other suburbs turned out to be in Mexico at the time of the Brown's massacre.

But no lead was too insignificant to check. In the western suburb of Naperville, police were summoned to a Brown's restaurant after a male customer threatened to stuff employees into a cooler "just like in Palatine" if they didn't give him a free chicken dinner. The man, who had been drinking, apparently was just upset because he had not received a biscuit with his meal. But he, too, was reviewed and then cleared as a suspect.

Another lead caught the attention of the public when it was leaked to the media two weeks after the murders. According to press reports, Palatine investigators issued a bulletin to law enforcement agencies saying they were looking for three men.

One was described as black-haired, six feet eight inches tall and weighing three hundred pounds, wearing a long black leather jacket and a shoulder holster. A second was described as six feet one inch tall and two hundred pounds, with slicked-back hair, and who fidgeted with a knife as he talked. There was little description of the third man. A tipster had told authorities that he had seen the three men having an argument with Brown's owner Richard Ehlenfeldt about a week before the murders.

Deputy Chief Gasior, in a news conference outside the restaurant, said that the murder task force had sent a confidential computer message to police agencies seeking help on locating these men. He maintained, however, the tight lid of silence on the case that had been imposed by Bratcher from the moment the bodies were discovered. "There are no flyers and no artist's renderings of any suspect being circulated by the Palatine task force," Gasior said defensively. "Our position is not to comment on people we want to question in this investigation, nor are we commenting on suspects."

But that lead also fell apart when the tipster was questioned extensively. He finally admitted to concocting the entire story. Police charged him with disorderly conduct for giving false information.

SEVEN

CHICAGO, IN A VERY REAL SENSE, WAS born with a massacre. It took place on August 15, 1812, when orders came to evacuate Fort Dearborn, the outpost on the banks of the Chicago River, lest it fall in the hands of advancing British troops. A group composed of militiamen, soldiers, and settlers and their wives and children left the fort and moved slowly southward along the river. They had barely gone two miles when Indian warriors daubed with paint fell upon them, and in the brief but bloody massacre that ensued, twenty-eight men, two women, and all the children were slain. As some made their escape, Captain William Wells, though badly wounded, fought on until a warrior named Peesotum scalped him and then divided his heart with another warrior, both eating it in the belief that they would thereby acquire Wells's courage. That night, Fort Dearborn was set afire while Indians stomped and shrieked.

More than a century later, another Chicago massacre

would further define the city. This one took place in a
converted garage at 2122 North Clark Street, on the icy,
cold morning of February 14, 1929. The St. Valentine's
Day Massacre began at about 10:30 A.M. when four men
burst into the S.M.C. Cartage Co. garage, which was being used by Al Capone's rival George "Bugs" Moran for
various illegal doings, notably those of his bootlegging
enterprise.

Two of the men who entered the building were dressed
as police officers, and they ordered the seven men inside
the garage—six Moran associates and Reinhardt Schwim-
mer, an optometrist who got his kicks hanging out with
mobsters—to line up against a whitewashed brick wall.

Immediately the intruders opened fire, spraying the
wall and the seven men with more than a hundred bullets.
For six of the victims, the time of death was noted on
police reports as 10:40 A.M. Frank Gusenberg, a top
Moran aide, lived for nearly three more hours, even
though there were fourteen bullets in his body. Dying, but
adhering to that code of honor among hoodlums, Gusenberg refused to tell the police who had done the shooting.

But everyone knew. "Only Capone kills like that," said
Moran.

Regardless, in the weeks following the murders, Chicago was aflurry with pointed fingers, suspicions, and
countersuspicions. The local Prohibition administrator
claimed, "The murders were not gangsters. They were
Chicago policemen." A Cook County assistant state's attorney named Walker Butler fingered the Purple Gang of
Detroit, while one of his colleagues suspected a local hood
named Joseph Lolordo, whose brother had recently been
killed by Moran's North Siders.

Though a total of $100,000 in reward money was offered, the real gunmen were never caught. It is now generally accepted that they were in the employ of Capone, who was out to grab Moran territory. The shooters failed to get Moran, their intended target. But he was so frightened—"one investigator who interviewed him said that he was hiding behind locked and guarded doors, and in a state of mind bordering upon hysteria," wrote Sewell Peaslee Wright in the preface to a 1945 book called *Chicago Murders*—that he soon left town and later died of natural causes while serving a prison sentence for robbery.

The word *massacre,* so easily attached to certain crimes, is strange and disturbing. Dictionaries define it as "butchery—the indiscriminate, merciless killing of human beings in large numbers or a large-scale slaughter of animals." Author Will Coster has offered this definition: Murders of groups by groups, employing overwhelming force and performed outside the normal moral codes of behavior of the culture which witnesses it.

What happened in Palatine was, by almost any definition, a massacre, and eleven days after it took place, detectives arranged for a kerosene-fired heater to be brought to the Brown's parking lot to melt the snow that had piled up behind a row of parking spaces. The heater came from the Chicago Park district. It had previously been used for the benign purpose of blowing hot air under the tarp that covered the football field in Soldier Field, softening the grass in winter in advance of Chicago Bears games.

The heater was placed twenty-five yards behind the restaurant and an evidence technician from the Palatine Police Department as well as Park district employees worked for several hours clearing the snow and melting it in a search for clues. "This was an attempt at being very

thorough," said Deputy Chief Gasior. "The point is that
they processed the whole area." Unfortunately, nothing of
value was found.

The investigation appeared to be going nowhere. Chief
Bratcher remained tight-lipped about its progress and
about what information was being developed or pursued.
With more than seventy-five investigators assigned to run
down leads, many of them working in pairs, and increasingly aware that there was not going to be a quick resolution to this case, the task force was settling in for the
long haul.

Some task force members began looking back to other
mass murder cases for signs of hope, or at least something
upon which to hang their fading optimism. Most mass
murders, the investigators knew, are solved when the perpetrator commits suicide or is killed by authorities, eliminating completely the need for a lengthy investigation
and trial.

To some investigators, the Palatine massacre appeared
to have been the work of what are known as "spree killers." According to experts, these people tend to commit
their killings within a short time span without a cooling-
off period. Gripped by some sort of dark and bloody pas-
sion, they continue to kill until they are caught.

"With a spree killer an emotional buildup of some type
occurs," said John Douglas, a former FBI agent whose
groundbreaking research in profiling techniques led to the
formation of the agency's Investigative Support Unit.
"There's the background of a dysfunctional family, early
childhood problems, low achieving. Then finally something erupts. The dam breaks."

Two decades before the Brown's murders, the Chicago
area had been terrorized by a band of racially motivated

spree killers. A group of black Vietnam veterans calling themselves the De Mau Mau slaughtered four people in a Barrington Hills house on August 4, 1972. The killers had set out on the Northwest Tollway from Chicago on a random search for victims and wound up at the home of Paul and Marion Corbett. They forced their way in and executed the Corbetts and two of their friends who were there, Dorothy Derry and Barbara Boand.

In a five-month crime spree, the gang killed ten white people in robberies, home invasions, and random shootings. In addition to the four people slain in Barrington Hills, a family of three was murdered on their Monee, Illinois, farm and three men were killed in separate shootings along Chicago-area expressways—a college student, a truck driver, and a soldier from Kentucky who had been sleeping in his pickup truck.

But most investigators did not think the Brown's massacre was similar to this earlier one and they took heart in the fact that in 1993, only two mass murders committed in the previous two decades in the United States remained unsolved. One had taken place on September 23, 1983, when robbers entered a Kentucky Fried Chicken restaurant in Kilgore, Texas, sometime around 10 P.M. Five people in the restaurant, including four employees, were taken to a nearby county, where they were led into a grassy field and shot in the back of the head. The other occurred on December 6, 1991, when four teenage girls were executed in an I Can't Believe It's Yogurt shop in Austin, Texas. The store was then set on fire.

The random nature and brutality of what had happened in Palatine was one of the crime's most troubling aspects. There is a need in the wake of such terrors to put a human face on the deeds, to make the evil not abstract but real.

In seeking a physical form for their fears, many saw the pockmarked face of the area's most famous and fearsome mass murderer, Richard Speck.

On the night of July 13, 1966, this drifter who had been looking for work on a Great Lakes freighter broke into a town house on the southeast side of Chicago where nine student nurses were living. Armed with a knife and a revolver, he woke and hog-tied the sleeping women and then methodically strangled and stabbed eight of them. The ninth woman, Filipino exchange student Corazon Amurao, escaped death by hiding under a bed until Speck left.

After dawn on July 14, Amurao made her way to a ledge outside a second-floor window. "They are all dead," she screamed. "My friends are all dead. Oh God, I'm the only one alive." Her description of the killer and fingerprints at the scene fueled a massive manhunt.

A twenty-four-year-old high-school dropout, Speck was born in Monmouth, Illinois, but spent much of his youth in Texas. By the spring of 1966, he was wanted for questioning in connection with an attempted rape and murder in Monmouth, to which he had returned. He seemed destined to play the part of the fiendish loser, right down to his tattoos: BORN TO RAISE HELL on his left forearm, LOVE and HATE on his knuckles.

As police scoured the nation, Speck spent the next three days hiding in Chicago flophouses and then slit his wrists. He was taken to Cook County Hospital, where he survived. A doctor spotted the tattoos and called authorities.

Speck never denied committing the murders, but claimed he blacked out after a binge of drinking and taking drugs and had no idea what he had done that night.

In 1967, he was condemned to death, but after the U.S. Supreme Court outlawed the death penalty in 1972, Speck was sentenced to spend the rest of his life in the Stateville Correctional Center near Joliet. In a bizarre videotape made years later by fellow prisoners, he was asked why he had killed the young nurses. "It just wasn't their night," he said, and then laughed. Speck had died in December 1991 after a heart attack, but the memory of him was strong.

Was there another Speck out there?

Reading the papers did not allay any fears. The *Chicago Sun-Times,* quoting crime experts, suggested that the Palatine killers "would seem to be the type of criminals most capable of eluding police—calm, calculating and unlikely to blab." Bolstering that assessment was Dr. James Cavanaugh, director of the law and psychiatry department at Rush-Presbyterian–St. Luke's Medical Center in Chicago. Based on the available information, he speculated that the killers appeared to be "intelligent, calm in the face of stress, methodical, purposeful, and organized." He added, "These are the worst types of criminals to deal with. They tend to be resourceful and can develop ways to cover their tracks."

The possibility that no one would ever be arrested for the killings had begun to throw a shadow of fear over the community. In the back of everyone's mind lurked the same uneasy question: Where and when would the killers strike next? Criminologist Jack Levin told the *New York Times,* "The trail grows cold as the days and weeks wear on, and there is less and less reason to believe a suspect will ever be apprehended."

EIGHT

IN ALMOST EVERY INVESTIGATION OF A
crime that goes unsolved, there often is a tip or lead
that particularly perplexes detectives, stubbornly defying
their best efforts to authoritatively confirm it or to completely shoot it down. The Brown's massacre was no exception. For the task force, no single lead, tip, or clue
would be more controversial than what became known as
Lead 80. It would spur more heated controversy than any
other aspect of the investigation, even though it would not
become public until nine months after the murders.

It arose out of the arrest of Reynaldo Aviles two days
before the Brown's massacre on a charge of armed robbery with a semiautomatic pistol. Aviles had entered the
lobby of the Edens Motel near Cicero and Peterson Avenues on Chicago's northwest side and slugged the desk
clerk in the face while demanding that the cash register
be emptied. Police were called and Aviles was arrested
after he was found hiding in a nearby garbage bin.

The task force didn't get involved with Aviles until several days later when prosecutors in the Cook County State's Attorney's Office reported that he had reached out to them from his jail cell, claiming he had information relating to the massacre, even though he had been in jail at the time.

With the armed robbery charge hanging over his head, Aviles had a strong motive to cooperate with authorities because his prior criminal background qualified him as a repeat offender under the Illinois Habitual Offender Statute, a law that sets out exceedingly stiff punishment for those who repeatedly engage in crimes. If convicted of this latest charge, he could be sentenced to prison for the rest of his life.

Aviles told police that he was a member of a street gang called the Puerto Rican Stones and that after he was locked up, he had several telephone conversations with a fellow gang member named José Cruz. According to Aviles, Cruz had admitted that he and other members of the Stones were responsible for the Brown's massacre.

The information was passed to the task force, logged in as "Lead 80," and assigned to Richard Zuley, a veteran Chicago police homicide detective, and Vic Valdez, an experienced investigator with the Illinois State Police, both of whom were among dozens of officers from surrounding police agencies on loan to the Palatine task force. Zuley and Valdez contacted the Chicago police Gang Crimes Unit and obtained information on Cruz. They then went to the Cook County Jail to talk to Aviles.

Aviles told the detectives that Cruz was a high-ranking member of the Stones and that during a January 13 telephone conversation, he had admitted being present at Brown's when the murders were committed. Aviles said he had called Cruz from a public telephone and said that Cruz had told him that another Stones' gang member named "Gabriel" went to the restaurant to commit a robbery, but "there was a fight and shit had to be done."

Further, Aviles said he and Cruz had committed several robberies with guns in the months prior to the murders to finance a large purchase of narcotics. Though the gang members were mostly from Chicago, Aviles said they were concentrating their crimes in the suburbs, where the odds of getting caught were low and the likelihood of obtaining large sums of money was high.

The detectives decided to hook up a recording device to a telephone and have Aviles call Cruz and talk about the murders. Aviles was told not to talk to Cruz until a court order for the eavesdropping could be obtained. But on the day the recording was to take place, Aviles shocked investigators when he told them that he had "accidentally" telephoned Cruz and that Cruz had said he no longer wanted to talk about the Brown's murders. The taping was called off.

In an attempt to assess Aviles's credibility, Zuley and Valdez took him from the jail and drove him to the north side of Chicago to point out locations where the gang had committed their holdups. He led them to a Captain Video store and to the King David Bakery, where, he said, Cruz had held up the worker while he and other gang members waited nearby in a car.

Aviles also told the detectives that his girlfriend had a friend who worked in a Burger King restaurant on Chicago's north side. Aviles said he had cased the restaurant and had questioned the friend at length, asking when the restaurant closed, the number of employees at different times of the day, and the location of the safe.

Aviles reported that Cruz wore gloves to avoid leaving fingerprints and favored a .38-caliber Smith & Wesson revolver. Also, he said, Cruz usually carried extra bullets so that he could reload the weapon, and when he reloaded, he always pocketed the expended shell casings. In addition, Aviles said his father lived in Wheeling, a suburb located just a few miles northwest of Palatine, and that gang members often stayed there after committing robberies.

Clearly, Zuley and Valdez believed Aviles was providing information about a series of robberies that were committed in a fashion similar to what appeared to have happened at Brown's and at locations that moved progressively north toward Palatine.

At about this time, a witness came forward who said he saw a man standing inside Brown's restaurant on the night of the murders. The witness said he had attempted to enter the restaurant, but the man came to the door and told him that it was closed. The witness had provided a description of the man that appeared to resemble a member of the Stones.

Aviles's information was further corroborated when Skokie police officer Brent Fowler brought in the victim of the King David Bakery robbery. He was shown a group of photographs and picked out Cruz as the man who robbed him.

An arrest warrant for Cruz was issued and on January 25, officers in the Chicago police Gang Crimes Unit were told to pick up Cruz.

But as important as the arrest was, it was then that the first serious cracks in the facade of cooperation among task force members started to appear. Details of what happened next would vary and long be the subject of contentious debate. According to some, Fowler, Zuley, and Valdez planned to accompany the officers, but at the last minute Palatine deputy police chief Jack McGregor told them the arrest would not be made that night. When Zuley called the Gang Crimes Unit to pass along the information, he was told that, in fact, there had been no such cancellation, that the arrest would be made that night, and that members of the Palatine police as well as high-ranking members of the task force would be present.

Infuriated because he believed task force members were attempting to take credit for his investigative work, Zuley went home. But Fowler, equally angry, demanded that he and Zuley be allowed to participate. Permission was granted.

Fowler summoned Zuley to a police station on Chicago's north side, where the task force members and Gang Crimes Unit officers were gathered. By one later account, Zuley exploded when he arrived, directing his anger at Kevin Kavanaugh, an investigator from the Cook County State's Attorney's Office who was in charge of the group preparing to arrest Cruz. "This is bullshit, cutting us out," Zuley yelled. "After we built this lead, you tell us to go home while you pick up the suspect." He stood almost nose to nose with a silent Kavanaugh, shouting and accusing him of "grandstanding this investigation."

The eruption was over quickly, but it paved the way for increasing acrimony and mistrust among some task force members.

Cruz and another gang member were picked up and brought to the Skokie police station for questioning. When Kavanaugh and his chief investigator, John Robertson, arrived at the station, Skokie police forbade them from going to the interrogation room. Angrily, they departed.

At the outset, Cruz denied he was the man who robbed the King David Bakery worker, maintaining that he had been in the car while an accomplice held up the worker. When the interrogation was resumed the following day, Cruz buckled and said that he had held the gun to the worker's head and taken his paycheck. Cruz was put in a lineup and the victim identified him.

Charged with armed robbery and armed violence for that holdup, Cruz and the fellow gang member were taken to the Palatine police station for questioning. After several hours, both men insisted they had nothing to do with the Brown's massacre. The investigators, frustrated with the lack of progress, decided to go to dinner. They were unaware that after they left, task force commander John Koziol, accompanied by Kavanaugh's chief investigator Robertson, walked into the interrogation room where Cruz was being held.

Less than an hour later, they emerged and Koziol said that Cruz was not involved and should be sent back to Skokie.

When Zuley returned from dinner, he confronted Koziol, saying, "What did you do? You've only worked on two murders in your life!" Enraged, he went on: "You talked to him for twenty-five minutes and determined he didn't do the murders and it took six hours to get him to confess to an armed robbery. How many gang-banging, murdering, robbing Puerto Ricans have you ever interviewed in Palatine?"

Koziol stood firm and Zuley backed down. Cruz was returned to Skokie to face the armed robbery and armed violence charges. But the next day, Fowler and another investigator from the Chicago police Gang Crimes Unit went to talk to Cruz again. They attempted to trick him by suggesting that perhaps he was a suspect because he had been picked up on security videotape at Brown's or because his fingerprints were found there.

"Man, there was no camera in that restaurant," Cruz blurted. He then asked to speak to Zuley, who was summoned to the station and, accompanied by Fowler, sat down in the interrogation room with Cruz.

"Look, man," Cruz said. "I didn't do it. But, man, they didn't have to shoot them all, man. They just shot all of them. They shot five of them in one place and two in the other—and just for chump change—there was a fight and they killed them all."

Cruz told Fowler and Zuley that his roommates were responsible. Records checks showed both had recently been incarcerated in state prison, one for a shoot-out with police in Chicago. The two were picked up—not by Zuley and Fowler, but by Koziol and Robertson.

Koziol questioned them and emerged to tell Zuley that he didn't think the pair was involved in the murders. But Koziol offered Zuley and Fowler a shot at them in the interrogation room. One of the two said he had spent the night of January 8 driving around with Cruz in Cruz's girlfriend's car, a 1985 silver-colored Ford Thunderbird with four round headlights and Wisconsin license plates. This seemed to fit with another piece of information. At least one person had previously told investigators that he saw a silver-colored car with four headlights and Wisconsin license plates parked behind Brown's the night of the murders.

Still, with no evidence against either of the two men, both were released. And soon the silver-colored car link also evaporated when it was learned that what the tipster actually saw was a car registered to a retired police officer living in Wisconsin with his wife, who had been in Palatine on the day of the murders. When the tipster was later confronted, he admitted that he hadn't seen the car at the restaurant but observed it two miles away. Eventually, he admitted giving several false tips to the task force.

A separate investigation of the other tipster, who had said he tried to get into the restaurant of the murders but was told by a Hispanic-looking man that it was closed, determined that the information was fabricated. That tipster was prosecuted for providing false information to the police.

Talking about this crime, particularly when the information provided was false, was proving bad for some people's well-being. Four months after talking to police, Aviles was found dead in his cell next to a suicide note addressed to his girlfriend. The cause was reported as an overdose of theophylline, an asthma medication.

NINE

A S THE INVESTIGATION ENTERED ITS FIFTH week, the task force had pursued hundreds of leads, eliminating most of them as not productive or linked to the murders. And, for the first time, word had begun to leak out to the media of internal disputes within its ranks. The *Chicago Tribune* reported that "investigative sources said that at one point they were not allowed to put one possible suspect under surveillance. The order was rescinded, but investigators were told to conduct the surveillance on their own time, at their own expenses and without enough equipment, such as vans, to make it successful."

The *Daily Southtown Economist* newspaper was particularly critical, reporting that the task force had waited more than a month to begin comparing fingerprints found in the restaurant with computerized fingerprint files in Illinois and other states.

Unnamed law enforcement sources told reporter Gene

O'Shea that by mid-February only some of the more than 100 prints found at the scene had been compared with more than two million prints of convicted felons kept on state police computers. And none of the prints from the restaurant had been sent to a separate Chicago Police fingerprint database which contained 850,000 prints.

One law enforcement source was quoted as saying, "They could have the killer's prints and haven't run it yet. I don't know why they're waiting so long. This is something that should have been done immediately."

The blame was placed squarely on Chief Bratcher for the task force's "almost total reliance for evidence processing" on the Northern Illinois Crime Laboratory and suggested that the Chicago Police Crime lab was better equipped to handle the task.

"Bratcher has staunchly opposed switching labs and refuses to budge," another source told the *Daily Southtown Economist*. "It all has to do with power and ego. They don't want to be told what to do and aren't too keen on accepting advice."

Bratcher defended the slow process of examining fingerprints and other evidence as a way of making sure that nothing was overlooked. "I stand by the crime lab," Bratcher said, referring to the Northern Illinois lab. "It may not be as big as others, but it's staffed by professional people and they're doing it right."

And then, Bratcher uttered the remark that would later come back to haunt him. He said that any claim of delays by the Northern Illinois lab was "patent malarkey."

When pressed by reporters about dissension within the task force, Bratcher conceded that investigators had not always unanimously agreed upon an investigative strategy, but said there had been "very, very few circum-

stances where there's been a difference of opinion on the
tactics by any member of the task force." Bratcher said
the task force was steadfast in its purpose. "The emphasis
won't be let down in the fourth week or the fourth
month—God forbid it takes that long," he said. But if it
did, he added, "We're prepared to be in the saddle as long
as it takes."

Meanwhile, investigators were attempting to determine
if anyone outside the restaurant in the surrounding area
heard any shots the night of the murders. They canvassed
the area, questioning shop owners and people who lived
near the restaurant. The search resulted in one man, Zoltan
Berta, a resident of an apartment building located near the
restaurant. Berta told detectives that at about 9:40 P.M. he
had been awakened by what he believed was a single
gunshot. He told authorities that he kept listening for a
while, but when he heard nothing, he went back to bed.
In order to test whether Berta or anyone could have heard
gunshots, the task force decided to conduct a series of
tests that began with the stationing of officers at different
locations outside the restaurant. Detectives believed that
because it was so cold on the night of the massacre, any
drivers passing by would likely have had their car windows closed. Even someone walking through the super-
market parking lot across the street would not have been
in a perfectly quiet atmosphere. There was passing traffic
on Northwest Highway and people pushing shopping
carts, not to mention the likelihood that anyone outside
was wearing earmuffs or a hat. So other officers went
inside the restaurant and, using some tattered bulletproof
vests as a target, fired more than two dozen rounds of
shots. There were several test periods. In some periods,
only one or two shots were fired; in others as many as

four or five. In some periods, no shots were fired. Sitting in their cars outside, officers were instructed by radio when shots would be fired and they were instructed to write down how many they heard.

None of the officers outside heard any of the shots.

As a result of the experiment, Berta's claim was dismissed as not credible. The experiment, however, did explain for many of the officers why, at the time the murders occurred, there had been no 911 telephone calls reporting gunshots.

TEN

"WE NEED TO MOVE ON," JENNIFER EHLEN-feldt, the twenty-three-year-old daughter of Richard and Lynn Ehlenfeldt was saying. It was less than a week after her parents' deaths, only two days after they had been buried, and she and her two sisters were speaking publicly for the first time. "We cannot hinge on this moment until we find someone that did this," Jennifer said. "To move on, we need to deal with who we are right now and express our sympathies for the other families."

She and her sisters were all wearing light blue ribbons, the tokens of sympathy for Castro and Solis, the two Palatine High School students who were killed at Brown's. The ribbons, first distributed at the high school, had become a common sight in Palatine. On their necks, the sisters also wore gold cross necklaces, gifts from Fred Brown, the son of the founder of the restaurant chain.

Jennifer, the eldest, was the most visibly emotional of the sisters. She opened the press conference by reading a prepared statement in front of about twenty-five journalists. That took only a few minutes. The question-and-answer session that followed was much longer. With the police still reluctant to answer questions from the press, reporters were eager to get some quotes from, as one of them cynically and callously put it, "anyone who was close to the action."

Battling to remain composed under the peppering from the press, Jennifer and her sisters, Dana and Joy, recalled fond memories of "roughing it" on family camping trips, their determination to push aside fears for their own safety, and in what surprised many of the reporters, their desire to reopen the shuttered restaurant as a realization of their parents' dream. "I can't begin to say enough for the people who worked there," said Dana, who worked full-time at the restaurant during vacations from the University of Illinois, Chicago, where she was a student. Her parents viewed all the workers as a family, she said. "They loved each and every worker they had there."

As the conference wound down, the daughters were asked how they would continue their lives after suffering such a tragedy. "We will get through this because our parents taught us how to cope," Jennifer said. "They taught us how to survive and they taught us how to be strong and with that, we will."

It was a remarkable performance, many of the reporters who witnessed it would recall, in large part because of the sincerity of the sisters. They really did, for all the emotions of the moment, seem ready to "move on."

Others were not so inclined, not so seemingly brave. A palpable fear continued to permeate Palatine and neighboring suburbs in the days and weeks and months following the killings. "Everybody is afraid. My kids are afraid,"

Palatine resident Jemma Adan told a reporter for the *Chicago Tribune.* "Somebody is on the loose, and we don't know who it is."

Edward Demos, a local locksmith, saw his business boom. "Even people who don't need more locks want more locks," he said.

Parents said they were watching their children more closely, and those who once had only locked their doors during the night now began to keep them locked during the daytime as well. At Regina's Café and More, located across the street from Brown's, employees began closing an hour earlier on weekends. The sale of security systems for restaurants was reported to be on the rise. Jamie Weber, the night manager at Regina's, spoke for many when she told a reporter for *USA Today,* "Now we go out the front door instead of the back door. We are all nervous."

Michael McMurray, the owner of Brothers Barbecue in Palatine, said that the killings made him feel as if a trip to the garbage bin behind his store was a potentially dangerous walk. Ron Rudolph, owner of a Baskin-Robbins ice cream store, said he had installed a new steel security door and was thinking about putting in security cameras and a "panic button" alarm system.

Joel Caplan, owner of a gun shop in the nearby suburb of Barrington, reported that requests for a firearm owner's identification card, a precursor to owning a weapon, and sales of guns had tripled since the murders. His stock of aerosol self-defense spray had sold out.

In the wake of the massacre, police began holding security seminars for citizens and business owners. At one such meeting held at Fremd High School, Palatine patrol officer Brad Grossman, a crime prevention specialist, told teens that 911 was not a phone number just for extreme emergencies. He said that if the teens saw what they thought was a suspicious person or vehicle near their workplace, they should not hesitate to call police.

"I encourage them to call," he said, advising them to be careful not to divulge any information about job procedures to strangers or even classmates and to voice concerns about inadequate security to their employers. Most people believed the seminars to be well-meaning efforts to ease the fears of the citizenry and, perhaps, to prevent future crimes. But some saw the efforts as a means to dispel the increasing criticism being leveled at the police for their investigative methods and their relative silence about the crime and who might have committed it. And so, many of the seminars were interrupted by questions.

"When are you going to get the killers?"

"Do you have any leads?"

"Any suspects?"

Deputy Chief Gasior was called upon to respond again and again, saying at times to various audiences, "We fully recognize the frustration and fear in our community," and "We would like nothing better than to reassure the public, but we can't do that. We are not going to reassure them by giving them false information."

Mayor Rita Mullins said the murders added another level of fear to the standard concerns parents have about letting their kids out of their sight. She said her own children had worked less than a block from Brown's at one time. "Most families have a child or a relative working in fast food. But for the grace of God, it may have been one of my children," she told the *Tribune*.

"That seems to be their rite of passage into the workforce," Mullins said. "You are proud that your kids are taking on that initiative . . . They should be able to go to

work and come home and be good citizens and not have
the fear of being murdered."

Sam Vignola, the owner of a Brown's restaurant in
Rolling Meadows, said that the chain tells its franchise
owners to vary the times they deposit money or remove
money from their safes in order to deter robberies. Vignola, who said robberies had not been a problem for the
chain, called the Palatine franchise a "very high-volume
store."

In addition, Vignola said that the Ehlenfeldts, though
new to the restaurant business, were careful about the way
they ran their store and were concerned about the safety
of their employees. He said they often drove workers
home after their shifts. "I don't know that something like
this could be prevented, whatever you did," Vignola said.

Two weeks after the killings, an appearance of nor-
malcy returned to Northwest Highway, one of the busiest
thoroughfares in the northwest suburbs. In the days following the massacre, the street was clogged as drivers
slowed to a crawl to get a good look at the place. Many
leaned from windows, cameras in hand, to snap what
would be sad mementos. After a couple of weeks, some
gapers still cast fearful glances at the empty building. But
they no longer stopped.

The restaurant itself was shuttered and the parking lot
deserted during the once-busy lunch-hour rush except for
a lone Palatine police squad car parked next to the garbage
bins in back of the restaurant. It was a presence to dis-
courage the bizarre person who might seek a piece of the
property as a souvenir and to serve as a visible reminder
that police still controlled the property.

The *Tribune*'s Christine Winter described the scene:
"Except for that eerie quiet at what would normally be a

lively place at noon, visitors from another planet—or any other creatures equally out of touch—wouldn't even know that something out of the ordinary had happened here just by driving past the building. The flowers left in the snow by community mourners were not visible from the busy intersection of Northwest Highway and Smith Street.

"The funeral processions are over, Mayor Rita Mullins is in Washington lobbying for stricter gun control, and at a last-minute, late-afternoon press conference in the Brown's parking lot, the police announced that they don't much like the media.

"Meanwhile, it looks like business as usual as cars pull in and out of neighboring car washes, fast-food joints and strip malls on both sides of the highway. Only the fluorescent green reward signs hanging in local businesses offer a grim visual reminder of the recent events.

"The crowds have even died down at the Palatine Inn ('Thank God,' sighed one waitress), the coffee shop less than a half-mile down the street which became a virtual headquarters for residents and media trying to figure out what it all meant in the wake of the horrifying news. There were even booths available at lunchtime—no waiting.

"Over the weekend, a homeless veteran stood at the entrance to a grocery a few miles east of Brown's Chicken with a sign offering to work for food. But instead of following the usual code that dictates that drivers avoid eye contact and keep moving, traffic slowed as a number of cars pulled over so people could offer him donations."

ELEVEN

ON A THURSDAY IN APRIL, EPIFANIA CASTRO was already in bed and asleep when her husband, Emmanuel, came into the bedroom. "Wake up," he said.

He jostled her arm. Groggily, she rolled over. "Get up," he said firmly.

"What is it?" she asked, struggling to come fully awake. "Is something wrong?"

"On the news. Something about Palatine," Castro replied. "They found a body. I didn't hear all of it. The reporter said it might be about the murders. Come and listen."

With what had to be a mixture of fear and anticipation, Epifania arose and together with her husband hurried to the television in the living room. They watched the commercials that had interrupted the news. Once again, she felt hope rising inside.

Beside her, Emmanuel fidgeted, waiting for more information as he involuntarily recalled the night he had walked through the Brown's restaurant door behind the police officer. The television reporter began to talk, and the mere mention of the word *Palatine* triggered more memories of that horrible night. "I hear the word and I'm back in the Brown's Chicken looking for my son," Castro later said. "I want them to catch the right guys so they can burn them to their bones, burn them to hell."

The television report was frustratingly brief and devoid of detail: The next morning, Friday, April 23, Palatine task force investigators planned to visit a railroad embankment in the nearby suburb of Barrington, where a mutilated corpse had been found on January 18, ten days after the Brown's massacre. A mother and daughter who were tracking deer had found the body. There was no doubt it was a murder: the body had no head and its right arm and left hand were missing.

Why? Why now? What is the connection? Castro wondered.

But the reporter on television offered no answers.

"What does this mean?" Epifania asked.

"Go back to bed," Castro said. "I don't know."

After the corpse was discovered in January, authorities had determined that the man was a five-foot nine-inch white male between the ages of twenty-three and thirty and weighing about 170 pounds. The man appeared to have been murdered at another location and then transported to the railroad embankment in Barrington. There were no fingerprints because of the absence of the left arm and right hand. Both had been severed with what was described as "a very sharp instrument."

By the beginning of March, the body had been tentatively identified as twenty-two-year-old Dean Fawcett, a resident of suburban LaGrange Park. Fawcett had no criminal background, but he had been sued by a currency exchange for bouncing checks.

The new search of the Barrington crime scene was prompted by a tip and police wouldn't say what it was or where it came from. And so, on that Friday morning in April, task force investigators, along with detectives from Barrington, the Illinois State Police, and the Cook County Sheriff's Office, systematically searched the embankment of the Elgin, Joliet & Eastern Railroad, looking for shell casings, fibers, clothing. They were looking for any clues that might help them solve this murder.

Castro listened to the television all day, waiting for more details, more news.

Finally it arrived: one person had been taken into custody. A tipster, according to one report, had told police the suspect could be connected to the Brown's massacre and to the body found near the tracks. The media besieged authorities and the families of victims, asking for answers that authorities were not prepared to give, that families did not know. "We're working very hard on closing this thing up and before we make any statements, we want to have everything tied up," Barrington police officer Roy Watson told the *Chicago Tribune*. "At this point in the investigation, it is a lot of tedious paperwork. We're trying to move toward charging people with crimes and it takes a while."

Deputy Chief Walt Gasior would only say: "We are continuing to investigate leads. We are not commenting on the specifics of the investigation."

At the time the body was discovered in January, authorities did not suspect a link to the Palatine murders because the state of decomposition suggested the murder had occurred before the seven were slain. Now, at least one source told the *Tribune,* the location and date of discovery were the best links to a connection, fueled by the tipster's information.

Rachel Ehlenfeldt, Richard Ehlenfeldt's mother, heard the news on the radio Friday morning at her Wisconsin home. "It's frustrating," she told reporters. "It was one of the first things I heard on the radio this morning and we're anxious to find out more details." Yet she remained patient, saying, "At the same time, we realize that this is going to take a lot of time. I think the whole family knows now that this isn't going to be solved overnight."

Her hopes had been dashed before: the arrest of Martin Blake just hours into the investigation (he was released without charge); the arrest a week later of three Schaumburg men (also released without charges); and the tip that police were seeking another group of three men (which turned out to be a hoax).

Now she was willing to be patient, to rein in her hopes. "I think it makes it easier to look at that way," she said. "You don't expect to hear immediately, so you're not let down when the phone doesn't ring."

Adolph Priester, a former high-school science teacher who had known the Ehlenfeldts and their family for more than thirty years, was also used to the waiting game, though he found it irritating. "The only way I can describe it, and it may not be the best, is that it's been like having a sharp stone in my shoe," he said. "The stone sometimes moves to where you don't feel it for a while, then it's there again causing you unbearable pain. We've seen all of this before. Let's just hope this time they have this thing solved."

An encouraging development took place on Saturday, the day after the search of the railroad embankment, when

the Cook County State's Attorney's Office charged
twenty-five-year-old Robert Faraci with the murder.

Faraci had formerly lived in Barrington and had been
sentenced to six years in prison in 1990 for delivery of
narcotics and two years for forgery. He had been paroled
in March of 1992. Police said Fawcett had been killed
December 28, eleven days before the Brown's murders
because he had threatened to inform authorities about a
check-forging scheme involving himself, Faraci, and a
third man. According to authorities, Fawcett had been
made to lie facedown on the ground and then was shot
four times in the head by the third man while Faraci
watched.

Police found a telephone number in Fawcett's pants
pocket. "There was a piece of paper with a Ramada Inn
logo on it and two telephone numbers," Barrington police
detective Jack Humer would later testify in court. Next to
one of the phone numbers was a room number that turned
out to be at a Best Western Motel in Broadview. The
motel room had been rented from early December 1992
through early January 1993 to a woman named Nadine
Lenarczak. She was arrested on an outstanding traffic warrant and asked about the phone number. Humer later said
that she said she was acquainted with Fawcett and that he
had stayed at a Ramada Inn near O'Hare International
Airport while he was working a bogus check scheme with
people she could identify only as Joe, Brian, and Paul.
Humer said police found out Fawcett was missing. That
led to the identification of the torso as Fawcett by family
members who recognized the clothing on the corpse.

The third man, whom the police would not identify,
was being sought.

The crime had been solved, police said, by reconstructing the final few days of Fawcett's life after his identity had been learned. Police were able to identify Faraci as one of the men last seen with Fawcett and tracked him to an address on Chicago's west side, but they were too late—he and his wife had already moved to Clearwater, Florida. His wife told police he left there shortly after she called police to report that he had beaten her in late January during a quarrel over whether he would drive her to her job as a waitress. Finally, police found and arrested him at the LP Motel in Norridge, a suburb abutting Chicago's northwest side. Faraci was arrested as he dined with three other people, one of whom was his wife, Rose.

Palatine task force members would not say whether Faraci's arrest put them any closer to solving the Brown's massacre. Cook County state's attorney Jack O'Malley said, "We haven't ruled these people out. However, we have not filed any charges against them in connection with Palatine."

Still, one police source told the *Chicago Sun-Times,* "These are two of the most brutal crimes in the history of the northwest suburbs. It defies common sense not to think that there could be a connection."

TWELVE

THE MEDIA FRENZY REACHED A NEAR FEVER pitch when police disclosed that Faraci had implicated himself and an associate in the Brown's massacre—and that Palatine police had the associate in custody.

Faraci told detectives during a marathon interrogation at the Barrington Police Department that he and eighteen-year-old Paul Modrowski had gone into Brown's just before closing time, and after they robbed the restaurant, Modrowski just started shooting. Faraci said he left the restaurant and ran to a car where a third man waited. "That crazy SOB killed everybody in there," Faraci recalled telling his accomplice.

Detectives arrested Modrowski for a traffic violation on Chicago's south side near his grandparents' home after tracking him there by using a wiretap on his parents' telephone. The officers picked him up on an outstanding arrest warrant that had been issued earlier after he failed to appear in court on January 19 on theft and burglary

charges in neighboring DuPage County—a day after Fawcett's body was discovered along the railroad embankment.

The parallels between the two crimes were apparent,
though not exact. Fawcett had been made to lie down
before he was killed with multiple gunshots. His head,
hands, and one arm had been removed with a saw and the
body parts were taken from the scene in an attempt to
prevent identification. The seven victims at Brown's were
also killed with multiple gunshots and Lynn Ehlenfeldt's
throat was cut. The killers, police believed, had taken
some steps to clean up the crime scene to prevent detec-
tion, including mopping up blood and collecting shell casings.

The mass of reporters surrounding the task force headquarters went into a near convulsion shortly before 4 P.M.
on April 28, 1993 when a silver-colored car drove inside
the building. A detective was spotted escorting a man out
of the car. He had a red coat pulled over his head. Authorities refused to identify him.

Reporters tracked down neighbors of the Faracis in
Clearwater. They said Faraci had left in a rush at the end
of March, leaving some belongings behind. One resident
said Faraci drove away in a blue Camaro pulling a U-
Haul trailer.

Modrowski, who had been living in Mokena, an Illinois
town fifty miles south of Palatine, was described as an unusual teenager who dressed in black jeans, black heavy-
metal T-shirts, and black, fingerless gloves. He used
several aliases, including Viktor Himler and Karl Schmidt,
and asked his friends to call him "Satan." The *Chicago
Tribune* quoted a high-school acquaintance as saying
Modrowski walked with a "stiff-legged Frankenstein-like

gait," and when he walked down the school hallways, "people would spread out to get out of his way.' "

Another former classmate said Modrowski once grabbed another teenager and held him down while drawing swastikas on his forehead with a marking pen. A police source told the *Chicago Sun-Times* that Modrowski was a "white supremacist" and other detectives said a search of Modrowski's grandparents' home turned up Nazi literature.

Fawcett and Modrowski had been jointly accused of wrongdoing in the past. Two years earlier, they were accused of stealing three checks, totaling $2,556, from Modrowski's mother, Linda, and attempting to cash them. Fawcett had been placed on court supervision and fined $90. And later that month, officers of the La Grange Park Police Department arrested Modrowski and Fawcett on a suspicion of burglarizing a home. Neither, however, was charged with the crime.

Initially, some detectives were skeptical of Faraci's story about the Brown's murders, but then a third person—whom police would not identify—corroborated the information. Still task force investigators were proceeding slowly, mindful of the previous Martin Blake incident and worried about the potential sting of media criticism.

Deputy Chief Gasior continued his closemouthed policy and refused to comment on the progress of the investigation. He would say only, "Any piece of information, however obscure or oblique on its face, is always incorporated into our database and compared against all the information we know." State's Attorney O'Malley repeated his statement from the previous day: "We haven't ruled these people out." At the same time, however,

O'Malley's media spokesman Andy Knott was less optimistic. He discounted a newspaper article that suggested police were searching for a twenty-year-old serial killer as "mere speculation of the rankest kind." And asked if the Palatine murders were about to be solved, he replied, "There's no reason to feel that way right now."

Faraci appeared briefly in Cook County Circuit Court in Rolling Meadows before Judge Michael F. Czaja, who ordered him held without bond. Authorities said they feared that if released, Faraci would attempt to flee the country to Italy, where his wife, Rose, was a citizen. Telephone records at the motel where he was arrested showed six calls were made from Faraci's room. One of them was to the Italian consulate.

Following the bond hearing, Chief Bratcher held a media briefing, during which he said, "We will continue to be interested in the perpetrators of the Barrington murders," adding that the task force was pursuing leads arising from Fawcett's murder.

One detective, who asked not to be named, told the *Sun-Times:* "There is no question that Modrowski is our man in this Fawcett thing." He added that Modrowski was a "very promising connection" to the Brown's massacre, particularly because of Faraci's statements as well as physical evidence found at the scene of both crimes.

Privately, other investigators told reporters that the key break in solving Fawcett's murder originated with Faraci's wife, Rose, who came forward, saying she feared for her life. Later she would say that Modrowski had threatened to kill her and Faraci if either of them talked to authorities about Fawcett's murder. Police also said they had received information from a tipster that led them to

look for Modrowski as the triggerman in both the Barrington and the Palatine murders.

But while they were cautiously considering the possibility that Faraci had offered the information on the
Brown's massacre in an attempt to get leniency on the
charge of murdering Fawcett, some investigators believed
the physical evidence would help make the connection
between the two cases.

Still, no critical evidence, such as a fingerprint or an
eyewitness, linked either man to the Brown's massacre.
In fact, one detective noted, the gun used to kill Fawcett
was a nine-millimeter pistol, while the gun used in the
Brown's murders was a .38-caliber revolver.

On April 29, 1993—six days after the search of the
railroad embankment and after two days of questioning—
Modrowski was charged with Fawcett's murder. As investigators continued to interrogate him about the
Brown's massacre, detectives searched a garbage dump
near Midway Airport—not far from Modrowski's grandparents' home—for the nine-millimeter pistol they believed Modrowski had used to kill Fawcett. They also
searched trash bins near the home. But no weapon was
found.

Detectives sought records of telephone calls just prior
to and just after the Brown's murders that were made from
the grandparents' home and Modrowski's parents' home.
Detectives wanted to speak with anyone Modrowski may
have talked to who might have heard something of significance. "It seems that everyone's spirits are really up
right now," said one member of the task force.

The case took another turn the next morning when
Modrowski came to court for a bond hearing. His attorney, assistant Cook County public defender Debra Grohs,

accused detectives of physically abusing Modrowski and of ignoring his requests for a lawyer during his forty-eight hours of interrogation. She pointed out a fact that frustrated authorities: there was no physical evidence linking her client to the Brown's massacre or to the murder of Fawcett. Detectives had only the word of Faraci, she said, and reiterated her claim that police officers, using their fists, slugged Modrowski several times in an attempt to persuade him to provide information.

"My client does not want to talk," Grohs said. "He has not told them anything. He has been hit. He is in pain."

But when Modrowski, a well-built six-foot-two-inch teenager, came to court for the ten-minute hearing, he did not appear to bear any marks of violence. After a judge ordered him held without bond, Modrowski was escorted from the courtroom to the lockup. Before he went through the courtroom door, he turned to nod his head at Grohs and then he smiled.

In mid-May, Modrowski and Faraci, were indicted by a Cook County grand jury. Defense attorneys Grohs and Dale Coventry, an attorney representing Modrowski, demanded that prosecutors save all notes and police reports related to the investigation, including those made by members of the Palatine task force. "We have to have access to all the information that was garnered during the investigation so we can make a determination of what will be of value to us in our defense," Coventry said.

Grohs reported that Modrowski was "shocked and scared" by police statements that they were attempting to connect him to the Brown's massacre. "He's as anxious as everybody else to hear what they're saying about him," she said, adding that Modrowski told her he was not involved. "I'm saying my client is saying he is innocent.

He has not made any statements to police."

She blasted Faraci's statements to police about Modrowski's involvement in the Brown's massacre. "He's trying to get himself out of a jam," she said. "We consider Faraci a very unreliable source."

Cook County Circuit Court judge Sam Amirante granted a motion by Grohs to keep Faraci's case separate from Modrowski's. "I don't want them together for both of their sakes," Grohs told the judge. "I just want to keep them apart so there's never any conflict whatsoever."

And Grohs continued to rip the police and the media for speculating on Modrowski's involvement in the Brown's massacre. "This case should be tried in the courtroom," she said. "It sounds to me like all of this is speculation."

Meanwhile, Faraci's attorney, assistant Cook County public defender Vito Colucci, said he would move to have his client's trial sent to another county because of the publicity about his possible involvement in the Brown's case.

At the same time, Modrowski's mother, Linda Modrowski, added a surreal element to the case when she told the *Sun-Times* that her son, in a telephone call from the Cook County Jail, told her that Fawcett was not really dead. She claimed that Fawcett was alive and living in California.

Coventry and police discounted her assertion. "Paul hasn't said anything about this," Coventry said. "The only information the state and the police have has been the fabrications of Mr. Faraci and his wife."

Assistant Cook County state's attorney Michael Gerber said the assertion was "absolutely absurd. There's no basis for that whatsoever."

Barrington Police Lieutenant Jeff Lawler insisted the body was that of Fawcett. "We stand on our belief that Dean Fawcett is the deceased person," Lawler said.

As the prosecution and defense prepared for trial, Barrington police came under fire for their handling of the crime scene where Fawcett's torso was found. A source close to the Palatine task force told the *Sun-Times* that Barrington police had waited months after discovering Fawcett's body to make a thorough search of the area because they believed Fawcett had been killed elsewhere and dumped in Barrington. "They made a dangerous conclusion," the source told the newspaper.

Further, the source suggested that Faraci and Modrowski could have been arrested sooner had proper procedures been followed. Unspoken was the possibility that evidence linking the men to the Brown's massacre might have been found.

Barrington Police Lieutenant Jeff Lawler did not agree and labeled the charge "unfair sniping" and "absolutely wrong." He said Illinois State Police crime scene technicians and Barrington detectives had searched the site for eight hours after Fawcett's body was found in January. And Lawler said the crime scene was larger than five football fields and was covered with eight inches of snow. Bulldozers and other heavy equipment were not used, he said, to avoid destroying any evidence that was buried. He insisted that after the snow had melted in February detectives returned with dogs trained to sniff out evidence such as rotting flesh and metal.

The source told the *Sun-Times,* however, that the first extensive search of the area didn't take place until after the tipster had led them to Faraci in April. That search included Palatine task force members and turned up nine-millimeter shell casings, which were suspected to have come from the murder weapon, as well as a hacksaw, which the investigators believed was used to cut up Fawcett's body. Despite the verbal sniping, one thing remained clear: No one yet had been charged with committing the Brown's massacre.

THIRTEEN

A BUILDING IS NOT, OF COURSE, A LIVING thing. But buildings where death has visited create peculiar and vexing problems for those who own them. Places where people die violently become, for many, symbols of horror. These sites exert a disturbing power, attracting grieving survivors, gawkers, and others with more macabre motives.

There is a fence that extends along a portion of the west side of 2100 block of Clark Street in Chicago, near the Lincoln Park Zoo. It surrounds a piece of ground at the edge of a retirement home. It is the sort of city space that few ever notice. But this fence stands guard in front of one of the most famous sites in the city, a slice of soil that some now say is haunted.

This is the site of the St. Valentine's Day Massacre, as the 1929 slaughter of seven men by the gun-toting minions of Al Capone has become fancifully known. For decades after the crime, the lot contained a building that was a favorite landmark for neighborhood kids coming of age in the days of *The Untouchables* on television. On any given day one could find groups of kids staring at the two-story building with its Werner Storage sign, imagining past mayhem inside what was then the S.M.C. Cartage Co. garage at 2122 North Clark Street.

The old garage was ordered demolished in 1967, shortly after it was used for the filming of a few scenes for the movie *The St. Valentine's Day Massacre,* starring Jason Robards and George Segal. At the time, George Stone, the director of the Lincoln Park urban renewal project and the man who ordered the building's demise, said, "Generally we try to preserve buildings that are of historical significance, but this is something we'd rather not remember."

National Wrecking Co. got to work. Up in Vancouver, British Columbia, an entrepreneur named George Patey read about the demolition and decided he would try to buy a piece, actually many pieces, of Chicago's bloody past. Patey purchased a seven-and-a-half-by-eleven-foot section of the bullet-riddled north wall. The price has never been disclosed, but the bricks, all 417 of them, were numbered, packed in barrels, and shipped to Canada. Seven bricks were missing, presumably stolen by cops or reporters who were first on the scene.

Patey first offered the wall to a Canadian restaurateur, who turned him down, saying, "I plan to serve food in this place, and I don't want to ruin the diners' appetites." The wall became a traveling exhibit, but the public decried it. A museum wouldn't take it off Patey's hands, and eventually it was installed in the men's room of the Banjo Palace, a Roaring '20s–style saloon Patey owned. That place closed in the early 1990s, and in 1996, Patey and his associate, E. W. "Bill" Eliason, tried to auction off the wall. The bidding, they said, would start at $200,000. They got some offers, but none was serious. They later hooked up with an Internet site that offered individual bricks for $1,000.

On Clark Street, a few people who have passed by the site claim they have heard screams and machine-gun fire. Some say that animals seem to be especially bothered— sometimes barking and howling, sometimes whining in fear.

But perhaps no building attracted as much attention as the Milwaukee apartment building where Jeffrey Dahmer killed most of his fifteen victims. Tourists from as far away as Japan came to the site, and it was reported that some people offered guards there as much as seventy-five dollars for a piece of brick. When Campus Circle, a public and private partnership, bought the building in 1992, it hired guards and erected a barbed wire fence to protect the building. By the end of that year, the forty-nine-unit building had been torn down. "I was there when they first swung the crane," Shirley Hughes, whose son Tony was murdered in Dahmer's apartment, told the media. "And I rejoiced. There needs to be something positive there, something that won't be looking so sad or make you feel so sad."

In trying to determine what to do with the site of the Brown's massacre, many looked to what had happened at a McDonald's restaurant in San Ysidro, California, where on July 18, 1984, James Huberty shot twenty-one people to death and injured nineteen more in the nation's second-worst single-day massacre. Joan Kroc, McDonald's major stockholder, demanded the building be demolished immediately and it was razed in the middle of the night.

The lot was donated to the city, but there was still debate, and a subsequent six-year battle among those who wanted a memorial, those who thought there shouldn't be any reminder of the tragedy, and those who wanted the land returned to commercial use. Eventually, Southwestern College in Chula Vista bought the land, put up a building, and erected a marble memorial.

"Marble is hard. Marble is cold," Bertha Alicia Gonzalez, who lost six friends in that massacre, told *Chicago Tribune* reporter Louise Kiernan. "It doesn't mean anything to us. We needed a quiet place where you could be sad, where you could start reflecting and wondering why this happened, where people could reach within themselves to find something strong to avoid any more tragedies."

In the first weeks after the Brown's massacre, many people shared the opinion of Palatine resident Kim Branch, twenty-five, who regularly drove by the site of the restaurant on her way to work. "Every time you pass by, you envision it. You wonder what happened. It's eerie," she told Kiernan.

After the shootings, the three daughters of Lynn and Richard Ehlenfeldt, who owned the franchise, said they hoped the restaurant would reopen, but they were unsure who would operate it. Their feelings echoed the belief that surviving the tragedy and returning the building to its original state could be a source of strength to survivors. The decision about what to do with the Palatine murder site was to be made jointly by company officials, the Ehlenfeldt daughters, and John Gregornik, the building's owner.

"We want people to come to Palatine," said Ed Smith,

a friend of the Ehlenfeldts. "But not to see the Brown's massacre site."

"Tear it down," Emmanuel Castro told the *Tribune*. "I don't want to see it because it reminds me of my Michael. Whenever I look at that building, it dissolves my soul. I would like that building to be torn down, so I don't see any more where my boy died."

On Tuesday, February 23, 1993, Castro began a petition drive calling for demolition of the restaurant in the hope at least to wipe out the physical reminder of the massacre, if not its memory. He proposed that a memorial be built there instead.

That same day, Brown's president Frank Portillo told the media he wanted to keep the restaurant in operation. "I don't see any value in knocking the building down," he said. "I think it would be more advantageous to Mr. Castro, myself, and all the survivors to work with our state legislators to pass laws so we could have stiffer punishment for people who commit crime."

"Knocking down the store would just destroy the Ehlenfeldts' dream, which I don't think would be right," Portillo added. He suggested an alternative—donating the first week's proceeds of the reopened restaurant to a scholarship fund at Palatine High School in memory of Michael Castro and Rico Solis. "And no matter what we do, when we pass that intersection, the survivors and myself are going to feel terrible. There is nothing we could put on that site that could make us feel good when we pass it," Portillo said.

In February, a cleaning crew had scrubbed away blood, disinfected the restaurant, and threw everything inside into the garbage, including still-remaining cartons of food and protective garments that had been used in the cleanup. The keys to the building were then given to the Ehlenfeldt sisters.

Emmanuel Castro modified his position, saying that he would not mind if the restaurant was torn down and replaced with a new building nearby. "They can reopen it ten yards away," he said. "As long as it's not on the same spot. Maybe I'll be their first customer."

FOURTEEN

ON AUGUST 9, 1993, THE NOON RUSH WAS JUST about over at a McDonald's restaurant in Kenosha, a Wisconsin town situated near the Illinois border, some fifty miles northeast of Palatine, when twenty-six-year-old Dion Terres stepped out of his car in the parking lot. He left the keys in the ignition, locked the door, and slammed it shut, realizing too late that the clip for the AR-15 semiautomatic assault rifle he was holding was sitting on the front seat. Apparently forgetting that he had another clip in his pocket, Terres left the rifle on the pavement next to the car. Clad in a blue football jersey and camouflage pants, he adjusted his red Oakley sunglasses and headed for the door. At his side, clutched in his right hand, was a stainless-steel .44-caliber Magnum pistol.

Inside, retired police captain Dan Collins put his cup of coffee and hamburger on a table and headed to the bathroom to wash up, offering a passing smile to another customer, Sandy Kenaga, who was taking a lunch break from her job as a hair salon manager. Nearby was a smattering of other customers—some standing in line, others at tables and in booths—when Terres walked in and fired a single warning shot into the ceiling.

Later, accounts would differ on what he actually said. Some heard, "Everybody get out!" Others believe Terres shouted, "Everybody get down!" What is clear is that the combination of the gunshot and the shouts triggered a mass panic. Some customers fled for the doors. Others, screaming, dove under the tables. That's when Terres began shooting.

His first shot grazed eighteen-year-old Kirk Hauptmann on the arm as he dashed for the door. Bleeding, he bolted across the parking lot to summon help. Inside, the pistol roared again and Kenaga crumpled to the floor, shot fatally in the back. The pistol fired again, and fifty-year-old Bruce Bojesen, a carpenter who had stopped for lunch while running an errand for his mother, was shot in the head. He was dead when he hit the floor.

Inside the bathroom, Collins removed his shoelaces, tied the stall door shut, and stood on the toilet so he would not be seen if someone came in. He smelled gun smoke coming through the vents. After a pause, there was a fourth shot and then silence. Minutes later, police came in and escorted him from the restaurant. On his way out, Collins saw Terres lying in a widening pool of blood. With the fourth shot, Terres had committed suicide. Witnesses said he stuck the pistol in his mouth and pulled the trigger. The gun was on the floor, just inches from Terres's hand.

Within hours, the call came in to the Brown's task force, sending a team of investigators speeding north toward Kenosha on Interstate 94. As they drove, a question loomed large: Could the Brown's massacre killer be lying dead on the tile of a McDonald's restaurant there? Or would this turn out to be another dead end?

They had been down this road before. Earlier in the year, police in Crystal Lake, a suburb about twenty miles north of Palatine, called the task force to report that an Arby's had been robbed during the night. One gunman had pulled off the heist after forcing four workers into the cooler. No one was hurt, the detective said. Perhaps, he added, the task force should send someone up right away.

That call had sent a new current of energy through the task force. The robbery at the Arby's had occurred late in the evening when a man wearing a mask walked in the door and drew a nine-millimeter semiautomatic pistol. He herded the four teenage workers into the cooler and escaped, with $1,400, to a waiting getaway car.

The similarities between this case and the Brown's robbery had been intriguing. Both restaurants were on U.S. Highway 14, located in parking lots near shopping centers, several hundred feet from the nearest store. Both robberies occurred late on a weekend night and victims were ordered into the restaurant cooler. Still, none of the Arby's victims were harmed. But several task force members were detailed to work the case along with Crystal Lake police, and for several days, they had examined crime scene evidence, exchanged information, and attempted to develop leads. They made no headway until, three weeks later, a citizen called in a tip. The driver of the getaway car, the caller said, was twenty-one-year-old Michael Kittle, a resident of Woodstock, a suburb located several miles north of Crystal Lake.

A dozen more task force members were assigned to investigate Kittle, and three weeks after the robbery, detectives searched Kittle's home and recovered a pistol, clothing, and other items that witnesses connected to the Arby's robbery. They also learned the identity of Kittle's partner, twenty-two-year-old Michael Spearman, also a resident of Woodstock. Spearman was arrested and a search of his residence turned up more guns. No money was recovered.

Both men were interviewed extensively by task force members at the Crystal Lake Police Department, and both had been eliminated as suspects in the Brown's massacre. "There were obvious similarities except for the homicides," Palatine police sergeant John Koziol had said at the time. Kittle and Spearman were charged with the robbery and both were later convicted and sentenced to prison. And so while that Arby's robbery had been solved, investigators had found themselves no closer to finding answers in the massacre.

What particularly intrigued task force members about the Kenosha murder-suicide was that Terres had lived in Arlington Heights, a suburb adjacent to Palatine, until he moved to Kenosha. Their interest was furthered after the discovery and viewing of a videotape in Terres's car. The thirty-five-minute tape, recorded by Terres the day before the shooting, was rambling, at times almost incoherent, and unnerving.

He spoke of becoming the nation's worst-ever serial killer and of inviting his former boss as well as family members to his home so he could kill them. He spoke of Jeffrey Dahmer of Milwaukee and coed slayer Ted Bundy. More significant to members of the task force, he also mentioned the Brown's massacre.

But any hopes that the Kenosha murder-suicide would provide answers to the Brown's massacre were snuffed out by the end of the next day and the detectives were on their way back home, convinced that Terres was not the Brown's killer. "Based upon the information we currently have, there does not appear to be a link between the Kenosha shootings and the mass murder here in Palatine," said Palatine police commander Mark Fleischhauser. "There is no evidence to link them."

The fact that Terres mentioned the Brown's massacre should not perhaps have come as a complete surprise to or caused too much hope for task force members. Fast-food restaurants in the 1990s were becoming familiar killing grounds. Cities such as Kenosha and suburbs such as Palatine were examples of America's love affair with fast food: main roads offering a collection of every sort of franchise the country had to offer. But that convenience masked another relationship, one between fast food and crime.

The reasons for this were obvious. America's fast-food restaurants were more attractive to armed robbers than convenience stores, gas stations, or banks because such retail businesses increasingly relied upon credit card transactions, but the fast-food business is done in cash. While convenience store chains worked hard to reduce the amount of money in the till, fast-food restaurants often have thousands of dollars on-site. Gas stations and banks routinely shield employees behind bullet-resistant barriers, a security measure that would be impractical at most fast-food restaurants. And the same features that make these restaurants so convenient—their location near intersections and highway off-ramps, even their drive-through windows—facilitate speedy getaways.

The 1984 McDonald's slaughter in San Ysidro had the distinction of being the largest in terms of body count, but it was only one of an ever-lengthening list of such fast-food calamities. It was a roster that continued to grow throughout the decade, each entry possessing its own grisly details, as in this April 1994 *USA Today* story out of Gadsden, Alabama: "When fire department medic Ronald Gray was called to a shooting scene here Friday, he confronted a tableau of horror: the bodies of three young people stacked on top of one another in a restaurant refrigerator.

"But the horror was compounded when Gray discovered one of the dead in the restaurant was his nephew, Darrell Collier, 23, father of an 18-month-old. Collier had just been promoted to manager.

"He had been shot in the head, along with Tamika Collins, 18, who was working her way through college, and Nathaniel Baker, 17, working for money for college and to help his family. Nearby was Bryant Archer, 17, who had crawled to a phone to call 911, despite having been shot in the jaw, neck, chest, and arm. He alone survived."

The article, as did most stories about fast-food restaurant tragedies, went on to note similar bloody days, which from 1993 on always included January 8 and Palatine.

In his 2001 book, *Fast Food Nation: The Dark Side of the All-American Meal,* author Eric Schlosser wrote: "The most common workplace injuries at fast-food restaurants are slips, falls, strains, and burns. The fast-food industry's expansion, however, coincided with a rising incidence of workplace violence in the United States. Roughly four or five fast-food workers are now murdered on the job every month, usually during the course of a robbery. Although most fast-food robberies end without bloodshed, the level of violent crime in the industry is surprisingly high. In 1998, more restaurant workers were murdered on the job in the United States than police officers."

Those are sobering statistics, as is the following from the book: "In just the past couple of years: Armed robbers struck nineteen McDonald's and Burger King restaurants along Interstate 85 in Virginia and North Carolina . . . A dean at Texas Southern University was shot and killed during a carjacking in the drive-thru lane of a Kentucky Fried Chicken in Houston. The manager of a Wal-Mart McDonald's in Durham, North Carolina, was shot during a robbery by two masked assailants. A nine-year-old girl was killed during a shoot-out between a robber and an off-duty police officer waiting in line at a McDonald's in Barstow, California. A twenty-year-old manager was killed during an armed robbery at a Sacramento, California, McDonald's. The manager had recognized one of the robbers, a former McDonald's employee; it was the manager's first day in the job. After being rejected for a new job at a McDonald's in Vallejo, California, a former employee shot three women who worked at the restaurant; one of the women was killed; the murderer left the restaurant laughing. And in Colorado Springs, a jury convicted a former employee of first-degree murder for the execution-style slayings of three teenage workers and a female manager at a Chuck E. Cheese restaurant. The killngs took place in Aurora, Colorado, at closing time and police later arrived to find a macabre scene. The bodies lay in an empty restaurant as burglar alarms rang, game lights flashed, a vacuum cleaner ran and Chuck E. Cheese mechanical animals continued to perform children's songs."

FIFTEEN

AFTER LONG CONSIDERATION, JENNIFER, DANA, and Joy Ehlenfeldt decided not to reopen their parents' restaurant. "We know in our hearts that our parents want us to follow our individual dreams and keep working to fulfill them," the daughters said in a statement released by their attorney at a Palatine Village Board meeting in December 1992, less than a month before the first anniversary of the massacre. "I think it's a well thought-out, tough decision that the girls made," Palatine trustee Jack Wagner told the *Chicago Tribune*. "They did it with a lot of class."

The Ehlenfeldt sisters had spoken earlier in the year about reopening the restaurant, but in the end, they decided against it. "Whoever committed the crime took away an immeasurable amount from our community, but we should not let them take any more," said the Ehlenfeldts through their attorney, adding that their parents would be "proud of us for our determination to continue to reach our goals."

In response, Frank Portillo said he would seek to open a new restaurant in Palatine at a different location. "I was kind of hoping that they would reopen, but I can appreciate that they wanted to go on with a different type of life," said Portillo. "I've made the decision to reopen the restaurant in Palatine, not at that particular site, but at one of the new shopping centers on Northwest Highway."

On January 7, 1994, the night before the first anniversary of the murders, the Prince of Peace Lutheran Church in Palatine was packed with more than two hundred people. They shared common and tragic bonds: all of them were tied to the bloody events of the year before, which had, to varying physical and emotional extents, shattered their lives and that of the community in which they lived and worked.

Among them were family members, relatives, and friends of the victims; politicians desperately trying to restore the image of Palatine; law enforcement officials frustrated by their inability to solve the crime and by the almost constant criticism leveled at them by the press and the public; and Palatine residents, many of them still shaken, still fearful. After all, the killer was still out there. Somewhere. Perhaps, some speculated, he was in Palatine.

The event this night was a memorial service for the victims, and on the way to the church, many people had driven by the restaurant. None of them stopped, but most slowed down as they cruised along Northwest Highway. What they saw was a building dark and padlocked, its parking lot empty and still except for the random scraps of litter that skittered across the blacktop, propelled by winter wind.

What many did not notice was that the distinctive Brown's sign had been removed. Workmen had taken it down the previous day. It was only a coincidence, company officials would later say, that the removal occurred in such close proximity to the anniversary of the murders.

Also largely unnoticed was a wreath that had been placed against the restaurant's front door. Emmanuel Castro had ordered it in memory of his sixteen-year-old son. And though he had placed the order, he had not delivered it to the site. When it came time to pick up the wreath from the florist, he realized he did not have the emotional strength to deliver it himself. The florist drove to the shuttered restaurant and hung it on the door. It read: MERRY CHRISTMAS MICHAEL CASTRO AND COWORKERS—WE LOVE YOU. YOUR EVER-LOVING FAMILY.

As the florist walked away, he could not help but see a bouquet of flowers that had been left days before on the ground outside the restaurant. It bore a simple message: IN LOVING MEMORY.

At the church, some in the crowd shivered as Mayor Rita Mullins recalled the combination of horror and fear that had spread across the town like a blanket at the news of the seven murders.

But she also struck a hopeful note when she talked of the town's ability to quickly draw together and she urged everyone to remember the "seven beautiful lives" that were ended on that terrible night. "Palatine was a wonderful place to live before January 8, 1993, and it still is," she said as forcefully as she could. "What happened on January 8 was a random act of violence that shook its foundations but didn't topple Palatine."

What Mullins did not tell those gathered was something she had decided to do on her own with the new city sticker that was soon to be issued. "I wanted to do something without making it a big thing," she would say almost ten years after the crime, discussing that "something" for the very first time. "It was very private, but I wanted something in the memory of those who lost their lives."

The new city sticker was going to feature seven small stars, one for each of the people killed in the Brown's massacre. "It was just a small way to let them know that they had not been forgotten," she would say those many years later.

On the night of that first-year memorial service there were Scripture readings, songs, and prayers. It was called "A Time to Remember." Organized by local pastors, the hour-long service was filled with tears for the past, prayers for the future, and frustration at the present.

While the service provided a measure of solace, the lack of progress in the investigation was increasingly frustrating. Reflecting on the past twelve months, Portillo called it the worst year of his life. "I can't believe that people stopped coming in the stores after six o'clock," he said in an interview with the *National Home Center News*. For the year, sales were down about $1 million for the entire chain. During that time, Portillo ordered increased nightly patrols at his restaurants, the installation of cameras to the security systems already in place, and security training seminars for store personnel.

The investigation, authorities conceded, had come to a virtual standstill—reduced to a waiting game. The task force, which had numbered as high as seventy-five investigators at its peak, had dropped by June to fewer than twenty investigators. Now, six months later, it numbered only ten.

The task force had moved out of its office headquarters in the Palatine Elementary School building and into a smaller space in the police department. Quietly, workers had packed up the computers, fax machines, and telephones and had taken down the photographs and maps from the walls. "It's not indicative at all of the investigation," Deputy Chief Gasior had said at the time. "It was just time to move."

Village finance director Robert Husselbee had called it an administrative decision and not an indication that the task force was cutting back on the investigation. He said, "I don't think there's any feeling from our perspective that they're scaling it back because there's a decrease in interest, but we believe it's primarily because the leads are thinner than they were before and so is the number of people they have working on it."

In the past year, more than three thousand telephone calls had been logged—some of them from people claiming to be psychics and some from what could only be called assorted kooks who wanted authorities to hear their theories, no matter how half-baked. More than $130,000 had been spent on equipment and overtime costs. The $107,000 reward fund—most of it put up by Portillo—had not been touched.

And now the telephone tip hotline rang only occasionally.

Indeed, doubts that the case would ever be solved weighed heavily on the minds of the victims' family members. These doubts had been building almost from the moment the bodies had been discovered. After a year, some were so quietly outraged that they were constantly dissecting every step and what they considered every misstep in the investigation.

What if, some asked, the department had paid more attention to the missing persons report filed by the family of Michael Castro on the night of the killings? What if the bodies had been discovered earlier?

What if, they asked, the police had been more prompt in conducting a thorough canvass of the neighborhood surrounding the restaurant? Would they have garnered information that was fresh in the minds of nearby residents, information that later faded from memory?

What if, they wondered, the department had not focused so exclusively on former Brown's employee Martin Blake in the hours after the bodies were discovered? Would they have picked up some other clue that instead was overlooked?

These simmering questions and their attendant doubts about the investigation had been stoked even more when just weeks earlier Cook County state's attorney Jack O'Malley suggested that the massacre might never be solved. "The fact is we live in a free society," O'Malley said during a radio interview. "And people get away with, literally, murder every day. The point is, it doesn't become automatically more likely to solve the case because there are seven victims, as opposed to three, as opposed to one.

"People sometimes have this belief that because a crime is so outrageous and so sensational and attracts so much publicity that it's almost inevitable that it will be solved," O'Malley continued. "And that's just simply not the case. There are other cases involving multiple murders around the country that have not been solved."

Though he defended the work of the task force,

O'Malley could not explain why some leads were not followed and why area businesses and others were not questioned until a week after the murders. "I don't think you can automatically conclude that someone is to blame," he said. "I hope it will be solved. How can I tell you whether it will be solved?" He then voiced a belief common to the law enforcement community: "Murder cases, generally, if they're not solved within a day or a couple of days—the likelihood of them being solved diminishes."

These outbursts of criticism and pessimism had compelled Chief Bratcher to call a news conference on the morning before the memorial service. It was his intention to answer the critics and dispel what had become a mountain of skepticism. "We will solve this case," Bratcher said as he stood behind a row of twenty-two eight-inch-thick three-ring binders holding thousands of police and forensic reports, computer files, and notes of interviews. He was flanked by a group of investigators from the Cook County Sheriff's Office, the FBI, and the State's Attorney's Office. "We are in this for the long haul . . . The case is still open," Bratcher concluded. "We still continue to investigate it. It isn't solved."

Patrick O'Brien, an assistant Cook County state's attorney who for a time had served as a legal adviser to the task force, pointed out to reporters that the investigation was particularly stymied by the lack of witnesses. "We had seven witnesses to an armed robbery and those seven witnesses were taken away from us," he said.

In what some considered a long-overdue decision, investigators began to provide new details of the crime. Many of these details had, through leaks to the press, already become public knowledge. But the police hoped that delivering them in this official manner might revitalize the stalled investigation. It was, in a sense, meant to be a plea to someone who might come forward with valuable information, perhaps even one of those who had taken part in the massacre. "We believe there is one person involved who didn't want to happen what happened," said Palatine police sergeant John Koziol.

Bratcher concurred. "We feel that there is, without question, someone who has information that we need, either an accessory, or someone the killers have talked to." Although no one came forward in the ensuing weeks, Bratcher had no idea how close to the truth he really was when he spoke these words.

THE "OFFICIAL INFORMATION" PROVIDED BY INVEStigators began with the restaurant's last receipt, which was time-stamped at 9:08 P.M., for a chicken dinner, rolls, and a soda. The receipt was for five dollars. A drink cup that had never been filled was found on the counter. At that time, Bratcher said, Lynn Ehlenfeldt, who kept the books, was probably tabulating the day's take. As she worked, Guadalupe Maldonado and Marcus Nellsen were cleaning the vats of cooking oil. Rico Solis and Michael Castro were mopping the floor, wiping down the wood-grain Formica tables, washing dishes in the kitchen, and hauling bags of trash through the unlocked side door.

In the walk-in cooler, Richard Ehlenfeldt and Thomas Mennes were boxing up the unsold chicken. The holdup was already in progress when they learned of it because Ehlenfeldt's credit card was found inside a box of chicken and Mennes's watch was discovered behind a stack of boxes.

Maldonado, Solis, Castro, and Nellsen were marched into the twenty-eight-degree smaller freezer. It was there that Castro was stabbed in the abdomen and Nellsen was hit on the head. All four were forced to sit or kneel on the floor.

Then, Lynn Ehlenfeldt was forced to open the safe, where she had already put the night's cash. This is when her throat was cut, either because she was frightened and confused and didn't follow directions or because she just didn't act quickly enough. The safe's bottom compartment, which contained about $300 in change and single dollar bills, was not rifled, even though it was open.

Along with the other four, Lynn Ehlenfeldt was put into the freezer, where at least twelve shots were fired. The killers then moved to the cooler where at least five shots were fired at Richard Ehlenfeldt and Mennes. Two bullets hit the walls and a third was discovered in the ceiling. Police believed at least twenty shots were fired in all. All the bullets had identical rifling marks, indicating they were all fired from the same gun. For investigators, the determination that only one gun was used was particularly significant—to fire twenty shots, the killers had to reload the weapon three times—an action that reinforced the cold-blooded nature of the massacre.

There were no shell casings, suggesting that the killers collected them. A mop had been pulled across the bloody floor and left leaning against the counter, either in an attempt to keep from stepping into blood or to clean blood off a shoe.

As they were leaving, the killers stopped at a gray electrical box near the side door and began flipping switches. They cut the electricity to the wall clock, stopping it at 9:50 P.M.

Further, Bratcher reported, investigators had lifted more than two hundred fingerprints from inside the restaurant, about twenty of which could not be matched to the victims. He said there was a good possibility that these belonged to the killers. But a national computer search conducted on the prints had failed to produce a match.

Bratcher conceded that despite thousands of hours of investigation, hundreds of interviews conducted in scores of cities across the nation, and dozens of ballistics tests performed on guns seized in armed robberies from the Chicago area and several other states, what was needed most was some kind of break. "Some of the evidence we've gathered may bear fruit, but all you need is just one small break; one phone call sometimes will do it," he said.

In the end, though, Bratcher could not answer the key question of the day, of the year: Why haven't the killers been caught?

Responding with a mixture of defensiveness and forthrightness, he said, "We won't know if we made a mistake until we catch someone."

SIXTEEN

AFTER A $500,000 RENOVATION, THE RESTAU-
rant building reopened to the public in October
1994 as a dry-cleaning business called Signature Cleaners.
Despite sweet rolls and politicians speaking in upbeat
tones, there was still a somber feeling to the ribbon cutting, as if those present were treading on hallowed ground.
One of the new partners in the venture, Don Bennish, said,
"We're trying to create a whole new business." Still, he
conceded, "I don't think the stigma of the tragedy will
ever go away. And maybe it shouldn't."

There had been proposals to reopen the restaurant and
try again, to create a memorial on the site, and to tear it
down and pave it over for good. Ultimately, the desire to
have a business at the location won out. And so the walls
were torn out and counters removed. Over three months,
the entire interior was replaced except for the floor.
Steam-cleaning machines were hauled in and a new
counter was installed.

The politicians put on an optimistic face. "For us to say tear it down is to say the criminals are dominant," said Palatine trustee Dan Varroney. "The point our village wanted to make is the criminals are not in charge, the families and businesses are."

However, while the criminals might not have been in charge, they were still on the loose and the case was no closer to solution. In what was becoming a sort of psychological torture, hopes had been raised and dashed on several occasions in the past few months as some of the five hundred new tips and leads teased with promise.

Among these, almost with regularity, were robberies and shootings in fast-food restaurants. And even if the crimes occurred hundreds of miles away, the investigators checked them out. In late January, they had examined a shooting at a Taco Bell restaurant in Clarksville, Tennessee. Three women, including one who was pregnant, and a man were found shot to death in two coolers in the rear of the store. Authorities said they were killed during a robbery attempt that occurred after the restaurant had closed and the workers were cleaning up. The shooting paralleled Brown's in several ways—the victims were shot several times each, they were left in coolers in the back of the restaurant, the murders occurred during a robbery in which money was taken, and police believed two killers were involved. The shootings were discovered at 7 A.M. the following morning when a day-shift employee arrived to find the workers' cars still in the lot and called the police.

But no firm link had been established between this robbery-murder and the Brown's case, and that lead had become just one more to be filed away with the hundreds

of others until the day that perhaps new evidence might
bring one of them back to life.

In March 1994, task force members arrested two Chicago men—half brothers—after a partial fingerprint from
the Brown's restaurant was said to have been matched to
one of them by the Automated Fingerprint Identification
System, the computerized database used by law enforcement nationwide. One source told the *Chicago Tribune*
that investigators had found a "legal, positive match." The
men's homes were searched several times by investigators. But after three days of questioning and repeated de-
nials, both men were released, much to the puzzlement of
the public and the large crowd of reporters who was
camped outside the Palatine police station. Assistant
state's attorney James McKay insisted that one of the men
remained a suspect, but critics suggested that the comment
was a face-saving one. And that particular suspect's lawyer, Akim Gursel, told the *Chicago Sun-Times* as he escorted his client from the station: "He's free to go to
Timbuktu."

Questions were raised about whether the fingerprint
comparison had been flawed and whether the suspect's
rights had been violated when he was kept at the station
for seventy-two hours before being released. Relatives of
the suspect said he had never been to Palatine, much less
inside the Brown's restaurant. Deputy Chief Gasior found
himself in the familiar position of defending the task
force's actions. "I am confident both the constitutional
rights and department procedures were followed," he told
reporters.

In May 1994, task force members interviewed twenty-
two-year-old Angel Juvenal Lopez after he was arrested
in Nogales, Arizona, on a fugitive warrant charging him

with participating in the robbery of a Mexican grocery in Arlington Heights in December 1992—just days before the Brown's massacre. Lopez also was a suspect in a grocery robbery in north suburban Mundelein and in neighboring Des Plaines during the same month. The detectives talked to him even though they really didn't believe Lopez was their man. "We have reason to believe he was not even in the country," said John Koziol, who had been promoted to the rank of Palatine police commander. "We believe he fled before the Brown's murders. But, in a case of this magnitude, we have to tie up all the loose ends."

The interview confirmed their suspicion. "We've talked to him," Deputy Chief Jack McGregor said a week later. "We're satisfied he was out of the country at the time."

As the second anniversary of the killings grew near, families and relatives and friends of the victims still grappled with their grief. Emmanuel Castro told the *Sun-Times* that he could feel the ghost of his dead son, Michael, walking through the family home, and just before Christmas, he heard a dresser drawer mysteriously open by itself. "My son will keep coming back until the killers are caught," Castro said, acknowledging at the same time that even if the killers were found, his life had been changed forever. "We keep asking, 'Why? Why them? What did they do?' "

Castro's wife, Epifania, organized a memorial service for January 8, 1995, at St. Joseph's Home for the Elderly on Northwest Highway, just a block from the site of the massacre. She wore a black T-shirt bearing a picture of her dead son and joined about 150 people who gathered to remember and to pray. "Every day a little piece of me gives loose, and I want to just believe it never happened," she said. "But then I get strength from above and go on.

My strength comes from my son because he's still a large part of my life."

Joy McClain could think only about what might have been as she prayed with the others. Before he was murdered, her fiancé, Marcus Nellsen, had proposed that they be married in the spring of 1995. After the murders, she had quit her job because too many well-intentioned friends and acquaintances constantly asked her about the latest developments in the case. She said she had stopped reading newspapers and watching television news—every murder case reminded her of the Brown's massacre.

As the day she was to be married approached, McClain found herself in even more pain. "It would have been the happiest day of my life," she said. "But now all I have is the thought of what it could have been and that I can't forget about him."

Jerry Mennes, who lost his twin brother in the massacre, could not bring himself to attend the memorial service. His wife, Diane, told reporters, "He's mad because they can't find the killer. I'm mad because my husband is mad. We just want to get on with our lives. We can't because they can't catch him."

More than a dozen detectives held a vigil of their own, coming to work to sit by the phones just in case the anniversary triggered a tip. But there were no calls.

As the case moved into the third year without anyone being charged with the murders, a backward look showed how the momentum of the search had faded. Calls for gun control, voiced right after the murders by Mayor Rita Mullins and Chicago mayor Richard Daley, had failed to inspire new legislation.

Frank Portillo continued to pressure elected officials to enact laws that would impose harsher penalties on robbers armed with guns who commit crimes in designated retail districts. But nothing had been done. Looking for ways to be more active in educating the public on laws concerning crime, and how state representatives vote on these issues, Portillo began putting up bulletin boards in all of his restaurants, each one containing a notice that listed the name of that area's state legislators, how they voted on issues of taxes and violent crime, information about how much money the state allocated for public protection, and a newsletter from the Chicago Crime Commission that explained how the average citizen could become involved.

Portillo announced that the notices also would be posted in a new Brown's Chicken restaurant scheduled to open in Palatine on February 1 just a mile away from the 1993 murder site. Despite that moment of optimism, beneath the surface, frustration bubbled. For a man such as Portillo—a successful entrepreneur who was used to making things happen—the failure of the task force to catch the killers nagged at him constantly. As the year 1995 began, he was determined that it would be a year of decisive action.

SEVENTEEN

I T HAD BEEN 6 A.M. EXACTLY, OR A MINUTE OR TWO after, on the icy morning of January 9, 1993, when the phone rang. Frank Portillo picked up the receiver in his home in Lombard, saying hello softly so as not to wake his wife, Joan. He immediately recognized the voice on the other end. It was Jeff Zavoral, a field supervisor with his company, saying, "Turn on the TV. You've got a problem in Palatine."

"And that's what I did," said Portillo, almost a decade later, the memory of that morning, and most of what would follow, still fresh in his mind. "It was on every channel, the morning news. So I got dressed and called my vice president, Tom Kennefick, and told him I'd be over to pick him up. We drove to Palatine in about forty-five minutes. We went to the restaurant, but it was cordoned off—the police wouldn't let us in.

"So we went to the police station," he recalled.

He did what he could there, talking with Mayor Mul-

lins and others, desperate for details and devastated when
they began to emerge.

Even a decade later, he still had difficulty retelling the
story. "We went to the police station," he repeated, pausing to control his emotions. His wife, Joan, grabbed his
arm with loving familiarity. They have known each other
for more than a half century, meeting when he was eighteen and she sixteen, and they have been together, through
the good times and the bad, ever since.

He was born the second child of Frank Portillo Sr.,
who had come to Chicago from Durango, Mexico, when
he was sixteen, and grew up poor with his family in the
area of Chicago now known as Cabrini-Green. It was
there that Frank Sr. met and married Beulah Docas, who
had come from Greece.

Frank Jr. fell in love with Joan Valdivia in high school
and upon graduating took an entry-level job as a drafts-
man at the Northern Illinois Gas Co., working his way up
to field engineer. But since he had no college degree, that
was as far as he could expect to advance.

That did not jibe with his ambitions, and he was con-
templating various career paths when he was approached
by a man named Fred Brown, a chicken farmer and a
friend of Frank Sr., who hired the younger Portillo to
redesign a small restaurant he was running, a place called
Brown's Fried Chicken, a take-out joint in Bridgeview, a
western Chicago suburb. During the weekends and nights
Frank Jr. spent working there, he noticed with increasing
interest that the place was packed. After talking with his
wife, he pitched Brown on the idea of allowing him to
open a second restaurant. It wouldn't be in competition,
Portillo told Brown, because it would be twenty-five miles

north. Brown agreed and set a price of $1,000.

When Portillo couldn't come up with that amount, Brown agreed to loan him the money to get started and the pair became partners. A few months later, in June 1958, Portillo and his wife opened their restaurant in Elmhurst. It was tough going for the first three years. The family, which by then included three children—Cheryl, Jerry, and Toni—lived in a basement apartment under the restaurant. Handing out free samples and distributing homemade coupons, the Portillos slowly established a regular clientele. As sales at both stores increased steadily, employees started approaching Brown and Portillo about opening their own restaurants. The two men opened five restaurants in partnership with them, retaining fifty-two percent ownership. Says Portillo: "I was a young, cocky, smart-alecky kid; he was old and wise. We were a great team."

By 1963, Brown, who was twenty-five years older than Portillo and spent winters in Florida, was letting Portillo handle day-to-day management. He offered advice only when he thought Portillo needed it. By 1965, the franchise boom had started. Friends, family, and investment groups besieged Portillo with requests to open their own locations. He began franchising, growing the chain to one hundred stores by 1987. When some units failed to perform as well as Portillo expected, he obtained a three million dollar loan to buy back twenty-five of them; he sold others.

By this time his brother, Dick, was also in the business. Five years younger than Frank, he had also started modestly, with a hot-dog stand in a six-by-twelve-foot trailer with no running water. He would eventually own and run more than twenty-five outposts under the names of Portillo's Hotdogs, Barney's, and Barnelli's Pasta Bowl. The brothers were shrewd businessmen and fierce competitors. Competition from chains such as Kentucky Fried Chicken was intense. To gain an edge, Portillo began serving a family-size portion of pasta with each meal, renaming the restaurants Brown's Chicken & Pasta in 1991.

Then Fred Brown passed away on December 30, 1992. Less than two weeks later, Frank Portillo faced the biggest crisis of his life.

The Palatine Brown's, one of the chain's oldest restaurants, had been open twenty-seven years. They'd had just two break-ins during that time. It was one of the higher-volume stores. The Ehlenfeldts had operated it for only nine months. Because they were new to the franchise business, Frank went out to the restaurant about once a month. It brought in $850,000 a year in gross sales and it employed twenty-five people plus part-time help. He would know not only the Ehlenfeldts, but all five of the murdered workers.

"When people buy a franchise they buy a system," Portillo said, a decade after the massacre. "They haven't been in this kind of business before they want to be taught the system. The Ehlenfeldts were typical. He had been in the cable business. He knew business, but not how to run one, so he came to us and we taught him the system."

"I remember when we had meetings of the franchisees, Dick would ask the best questions," said Joan. "And his wife was supportive all the way. They were a lovely family. Frank says that's what being a franchise is all about. The whole Ehlenfeldt family got involved in it."

The Sunday following the murders, Portillo, along with Mayor Rita Mullins, village trustee Mike Cassidy, and a representative from Allstate Insurance, went to visit the families of the victims. Their first stop was at the home of Michael Castro.

"As soon as Rita introduced me, Mr. Castro started punching me in the face and chest, crying that he wanted his Michael back," Portillo recalled a decade later. "I grabbed him and put him in a bear hug, and then I felt his knees give out and he slid down and all he kept saying was, 'I want my Michael back. I want my Michael back.'"

Portillo visited all the families of the victims on that painfully emotional day. "I wanted to help them get their insurance benefits, the death benefits. But they had to wait until the death certificates were signed, and they weren't all signed. So I helped with that," he recalled. "I guess we worked that day from nine or ten in the morning to nine or ten at night. I was going on adrenaline."

Frank and Joan went to every wake and every funeral of the victims. The week took its toll. "The way he was going, I knew he was going to lose it," recalled Joan. "At the funerals I watched him go up to every family member in every victim's family and hug them and talk to them. Over and over again. Trying to comfort them. Showing them they weren't alone—that he was there."

The funeral of Guadalupe Maldonado was the last one they attended. They sat in a pew listening to the sermon, but what they would always remember is the sound of the dead man's wife, Beatriz, and her youngest child wailing throughout the service.

"That's the night, after that, that he really lost it," said Joan. Indeed, as he and his wife recalled that decade-old event, Portillo began to sob and his body started to shake. "When we came home he asked me to fix him a drink. I was surprised. He never drank. But he had a Southern

Comfort. We ate some popcorn. And then he had another drink. At two A.M. he called the priest who'd given the eulogy at Maldonado's funeral to tell him what a great job he'd done. Then he started to cry, to sob—deep sobs. I couldn't stop him. It went on and on and on. Finally, I called our son to come over. He's a big strapping guy. And he took his father in his arms."

"I made a promise to Mr. Castro," said Frank as he struggled to compose himself. "I couldn't help Michael, but I had to do something, spend the good part of my life to make places for people in the service industry, people who served the public, safer. I didn't know how, but I was going to do it. It was also a way to vent my anger. I never felt guilty, but I was so angry. I just felt this couldn't happen in this great country of ours."

He started with education. "I'd tell them things like not to go out and empty the garbage after dark, make sure your employees are aware of security procedures," Portillo recalled.

But Portillo had more serious concerns than educating employees. With the television news broadcasting stories about the "Brown's massacre" night after night and the perpetrator on the loose, frightened customers stopped coming to his restaurants. The business to which Frank Portillo had devoted his life began to teeter on the brink of bankruptcy.

EIGHTEEN

"FOR THOSE FIRST FEW WEEKS, ACTUALLY FOR most of that first year, it seemed to me that we were on the television news morning, afternoon, and night," Frank Portillo would recall a decade later.

Understandably, such press was not good for business. Sales had dropped 20 percent by the end of 1993, effectively wiping out his profits. "If they had found the perpetrators shortly after the incident, it would have been so much better for the survival of the chain, but the franchisees were suffering; they couldn't pay their franchise royalties—it was a disaster," said David L. Epstein, in an interview with *Fortune Small Business* magazine. Epstein, an investment banker, as principal of J. H. Chapman Group, said he stepped in to help Portillo manage the firm's finances.

Exacerbating Portillo's business decline was an exodus of employees who thought the massacre the work of a serial killer. He found himself trying to convince franchise owners and employees that the restaurants were safe. He contacted police departments in all the suburbs where he had restaurants and requested a squad car be sent to each of them thirty minutes before closing. "Every police department did it," Portillo recalled. "They made sure all the employees got out of the restaurants and into their cars. Then, during the day, they'd check on them. They did that every day for six to eight months.

"I went to the county police immediately after the tragedy and I had all my franchisees and employees and their families bring in police to give instructions on how to handle things, how to make the restaurant safer. In 1993, we became the safest restaurant chain in the U.S. We put security cameras in every restaurant. We put in other things, some I can't talk about because the buildings wouldn't be secure if people found out what they were, but it was state-of-the-art security," he said.

Portillo also became an activist on other fronts. He started a radio show called *Citizens' Lobby,* a talk show with the lofty intention of helping to make Illinois the safest place to live, work, and play in America. "That was the motto," he said.

His activism almost immediately began to attract attention. One of the people who contacted him was Robert Fuesel, a former investigator for the U.S. Treasury Department who was executive director of the Chicago Crime Commission. In late 1993, he invited Portillo to join the commission. Portillo accepted. Meeting and talking with other members, such as Thomas Hampson, a private investigator with a law enforcement background, and John Flood, then president of the Combined Counties Police Association union, Portillo began to wonder if more could not be done to solve the case. Based on what mem-

bers of the commission told him, Portillo concluded that
there should be more coordination with experienced homicide detectives in Chicago and that a statewide task force
should be set up to help small suburban police departments tackle major crimes such as the Brown's massacre.

Shortly before the second anniversary of the massacre
in 1995, Portillo was shocked by the news that Emmanuel
Castro was filing suit against the Brown's chain, charging
that the company hadn't done enough to keep employees
safe. Lawyers for the family of Rico Solis would later file
a similar suit.

"I was very hurt by that, and at that time I went to
Bratcher to ask him for just enough information to cover
myself against the lawsuits," Portillo recalled. "He said
no, that it was an ongoing investigation. I was not happy,
but by then my relationship with the police was fizzling
away.

"I was becoming a pretty vocal critic of the police by
then. But what they didn't understand was that I wasn't
criticizing the department so much as the system. There's
something wrong with the system, where small-town police who don't have experience have jurisdiction over
more experienced homicide detectives. I think they were
working as hard as they could. They wanted to solve this.
They just weren't qualified. Look at it this way: I'm president of fifty-eight restaurants. McDonald's has twenty-
seven billion or something. So do they come to me and
say, 'Hey, you want to be president of our corporation?'
I could work seven days a week, but I still wouldn't be
qualified. It's the same thing with a small town.

"For the first couple of years I thought the police were
doing their job," Portillo says now. "We'd talk once every
two months or so. I had someone on the task force I'd

talk to. He kept me informed. One day I said to Bratcher, 'I'm getting all these calls on Lead 80 and I'm hearing these criticisms of how your police department handled it.' He said, 'I never talk to civilians about an ongoing case, but in this case I'll make an exception. If you want to come and talk, we'll sit down with the key people.' "

So, in May 1995, a meeting was set up with Bratcher and other principals on the task force. Bratcher said no reports or documents would be turned over that might be used to defend the lawsuits, but he and the others would try to address Portillo's concerns without compromising the investigation. In preparation, Portillo had lengthy talks with his new pals on the Crime Commission and brainstormed with other law enforcement professionals such as Alan Master, an ex–FBI agent; John Flood, of the Combined Counties Police Association; and some investigators who had formerly worked on the Brown's task force. "These advisers took me under their wing," says Portillo. "They coached me on what to ask. I didn't know what to ask a chief of police."

At that May meeting with Portillo were Bratcher; his second-in-command, John Koziol; Jim Bell of the FBI, along with FBI agent Bob Scigalski, both of whom were task force members; and Patrick O'Brien, a Cook County assistant state's attorney who had been an adviser to the task force.

They met for four hours. Portillo remembers it as a contentious time, during which he asked pointed questions. He can still remember some of the exchanges. "I don't mean to be disrespectful," he recalled saying to Scigalski, "but can I ask you how many homicides you've handled?"

The FBI agent looked at Bratcher and said, "Do I have to answer that?"

"It's okay," said Bratcher.

Scigalski had been with the FBI for twenty-five years, but during that time, he said he had worked on just three homicides, Portillo recalled.

He said he later asked Koziol a variation of the same question: "I don't mean to be disrespectful, but this is a small town; how many murders have you investigated?

"I remember that he threw his pencil in the air and said, 'I'm no country bumpkin,'" Portillo recalled. "I don't think any of the men at the meeting understood how much this murder shook me up emotionally. My company almost went bankrupt, so I asked the questions. I wasn't interested in personalities or mistakes or egos. I was just interested in whether the police were doing their job."

Portillo recalled that he asked if it would be possible to set up another meeting, one that would include Richard Zuley, the Chicago Police Department homicide detective who had championed Lead 80. Portillo quoted Bratcher as saying: "I hate the fucking SOB, but I'll set up a meeting with Zuley."

Portillo said he went back to his office. "Bratcher had said he would set up the meeting in three weeks," he recalled. "I wrote him a letter and thanked him for the meeting and said, 'I'm just confirming that we're going to have that meeting with Zuley and you'll be ten feet tall in my book if you'll do that.'"

But by the end of August, Portillo still had not heard back from Bratcher about when the meeting would be held. He was increasingly frustrated and beleaguered. His company was falling behind on its bills. His lawyer and accountant had dropped him as a client, and his bank had put him in what was called a "workout," forcing him to sell stores to pay down his $3 million loan. Portillo liquidated other ones to raise cash. He considered selling the business outright.

He was a self-admitted basket case, sometimes getting out of bed at 3 A.M. and exercising on the Universal Gym in his house to try to clear his mind and, for a few minutes, forget his troubles.

NINETEEN

THE TRADITION OF INVESTIGATIVE REPORTING in Chicago journalism is long and legendary. When reporters get their teeth into a story, their tenacity is not unlike that of an anxious terrier with a toy. And the bigger the story, the fiercer their determination. That is one reason why Lead 80, long kept under wraps by the task force, exploded into the public eye in the fall of 1995, refueling charges that the Palatine investigators had botched the case.

Investigative reporters Chuck Goudie and Dave Savini, working for competing television stations—WLS (Channel 7) and WMAQ (Channel 5), respectively—broadcast reports that focused on the investigation of the claim by accused armed robber Renaldo Aviles that while in the Cook County Jail, he had overheard José Cruz brag about participating in the killings with fellow members of the Puerto Rican Stones street gang.

Savini disclosed the location of a vehicle that Aviles

said Cruz and fellow gang members had used during several robberies they committed, raising the question about whether there might be evidence in or on the car that might link it to the Brown's massacre. Goudie reported that Lead 80 had been ineptly handled by the task force and backed it up with a nine-page document that he contended was a report from the task force. It was a devastating indictment, purporting that Cruz had not only been questioned briefly and in a cursory fashion, but that several members of the task force had vigorously argued against his release.

"Toward the end of 1995, a confidential source called me and said something was bugging him," Savini said a decade after the massacre. "He had had something in a file for a long time that he thought somebody should see. He shared with me a copy of Lead 80. I took a look, read it, and was pretty shocked by it. It was a strongly written report that claimed to have incriminating evidence, not from the physical evidence standpoint, but through the interrogation and police procedure."

The reports made for great television and created a new round of finger-pointing and consternation. Among the most stunned by the news reports was Portillo, who had been frustrated in his attempt to meet with Chief Bratcher.

To defend against the lawsuit brought against the company by the families of Michael Castro and Rico Solis, Portillo's lawyers had subpoenaed detailed task force investigative reports and crime scene photos. The lawyers wanted the records to support their theory that there was little or nothing that could have been done by the company or its franchise holders, Richard and Lynn Ehlenfeldt, to prevent the murders. Portillo said Bratcher had initially agreed to provide some material to Portillo and his lawyers. But for reasons never explained, Bratcher had changed his mind, and said there would be no task force information provided, effectively bringing a close to their relationship.

By now Portillo was aware that the investigation of Lead 80 had led to Zuley's dismissal from the task force. Zuley had been most adamant and vocal about his feeling that the lead had not been adequately investigated. The dismissal came not long after an emergency meeting Bratcher called one afternoon. The meeting was triggered by a media report that contained information about the investigation that could have come only from a task force leak.

One member of the task force later recalled how this meeting occurred. "Pagers started going off," said the detective. "Everybody was called in for a meeting. We thought there had been a break in the case."

The room at the task force headquarters was hushed as Bratcher walked in and stood behind a lectern. "Good afternoon, gentlemen," he said, emphasizing that last word and then pausing for what the detective called "a long, dramatic moment." Bratcher then leaned over the lectern, scanned the assembled gathering of task force members, and said forcefully, "Someone in this room has made a career decision."

He went on to describe the information that had been leaked to the press and said he believed it could only have come from within the investigative ranks. When the source of the leak was discovered, he said, appropriate action would be taken. Days later and without any public explanation, Zuley was dispatched back to his regular assignment in the Chicago Police Homicide Division.

Portillo and Zuley grew close after his dismissal. "The

guy is brilliant," Portillo said ten years after the massacre.
"We love him," says his wife, Joan.

Though details of the Zuley dismissal were not part of
the television reports from Goudie and Savini, Portillo
believed he knew what was going on, and these reports
further fueled his doubts about the investigation. Coupled
with his recent estrangement from Bratcher, he found
himself increasingly frustrated. For the first time Portillo
began to publicly express doubts about how the investigation had been handled. But merely expressing his
doubts was not at all satisfying. He wanted action. He
talked to fellow members of the Crime Commission and
strenuously suggested it was time for them to join forces
with the Better Government Association and launch what
would be, in a very real sense, an investigation into the
investigation.

Founded in Chicago shortly after the Crime Commission, the BGA had been created in response to the rise in
power of Al Capone and the corruption of elections, politicians, and the government. Like the Crime Commission,
it is a nonpartisan, not-for-profit group, getting its support
from citizens, businesses, and foundations. It refuses fund-
ing from government and political organizations.

During the 1960s and 1970s, the BGA dramatically
increased its public profile by teaming up with reporters
at numerous Chicago news organizations to conduct a
wide variety of hard-hitting investigations that detailed
abuses ranging from vote fraud to political corruption. Beginning with an exposé in 1962 of waste and fraud at
Chicago's Metropolitan Sanitary District that was done
with the *Chicago Tribune,* the BGA partnered in several
award-winning investigations—two won Pulitzer Prizes—
with such news-gathering organizations as CBS's *60*

Minutes, ABC News's *20/20, Time, Newsweek, Mother Jones,* the *Chicago Daily News,* and the *Chicago Sun-Times.* One of its most notable cooperative ventures resulted in a series of articles in the *Sun-Times* about the newspaper's purchase of a tavern in 1977, which it renamed the Mirage, and how inspectors and other city workers had practically beaten down the door seeking bribes and payoffs.

The BGA was headed by J. Terrence Brunner, an outspoken lawyer who had served as an assistant U.S. attorney in Chicago and as a special prosecutor detailed to the organized crime division of the Department of Justice in the 1960s. He had joined the BGA in 1971, and under his direction, the group had established itself as a hard-hitting investigative truth-seeker. But there were some less-than-favorably-received ventures as well, such as its push for police to search for additional victims of serial killer John Wayne Gacy. That inquiry had been fruitless, turning up shovels of dirt and no bodies. Despite the successes of the 1990s, Brunner was often viewed as something of a publicity hound whose charges were little more than sound and fury with minimal substance.

In response to Portillo's call for an investigation of the task force, Thomas Kirkpatrick, executive director of the Crime Commission, said that the group and the BGA would meet. "We don't investigate murders," Kirkpatrick told the *Tribune.* "But we do want to make sure that all information in a very serious murder case is shared adequately and that cooperation exists among the agencies doing the investigation. We are taking the request very seriously. Our interest is to see that the public gets good law enforcement. If mistakes were made or issues interfered with, we want to know it."

Portillo kept a low profile while members of the two organizations met. But upon hearing of the possibility of this collaborative effort, Bratcher issued a news release that many felt was a preemptive strike against any investigation of the task force. The release particularly addressed the handling of Lead 80, saying, "The Palatine Investigative Task Force and FBI investigators conducted a thorough follow-up investigation into a lead connecting Chicago robbers with the Palatine mass murder case. As with all significant avenues of investigation pursued by our task force, this investigation has been carefully supervised, monitored and assessed.

"This investigation started with tips provided by questionable sources. Renaldo Aviles, a convicted murderer and armed robber facing mandatory life in prison, gave conflicting statements about alleged conversations that were materially inconsistent. When an attempt was made to overhear subsequent conversations, Aviles prevented it."

The release went on to note that the tipster who provided information relating to the silver-colored car allegedly seen in the Brown's parking lot on the night of the murders had pleaded guilty to providing false information to police and was sentenced to a year of probation and community service. "While the large investment of investigative time resulted in the clearance of other robbery cases, it did not develop a productive link with the Palatine case," Bratcher said. "I am satisfied with the course of this investigation."

Bratcher also tore holes in Goudie's and Savini's television news reports. "Assertions in those news reports that a particular lead was not thoroughly investigated are demonstrably false," Bratcher said. He said a considerable

portion of the document obtained by Goudie that pur-
ported to criticize the investigation of Lead 80 was based
on incorrect information and contained "several inconsistencies." He disclosed that Zuley had written the document and that Zuley had been kicked off the task force.

"Without going into the specifics of our investigation,
which we have refused to do with these or any other suspects, let me emphasize that there was not enough evidence to warrant arrests when we first questioned these
suspects," Bratcher said. "No new evidence has been uncovered or brought to our attention since then."

Patrick O'Brien, who had been assigned to the task
force in its early days in his capacity as an assistant Cook
County state's attorney, publicly backed Bratcher, saying
Cruz had been properly interrogated. Further, he said, the
FBI had been asked to review Lead 80 and the manner in
which it was investigated, and the agency determined that
it was handled thoroughly and properly. "It was not a
situation where somebody talked to him for 10 minutes
and let him go," O'Brien told the *Sun-Times*. "A number
of different questioning techniques were used, all the
kinds of hooks you throw someone to allow them to make
a statement."

"Lead 80," Bratcher concluded, had been "beaten to
death."

TWENTY

IT WAS THE STRANGEST KIND OF ANNIVERSARY gift, but in January 1996, three years after the Brown's massacre, Chief Bratcher held a press conference and offered a present to the media: details of the crime that had long been kept secret. It was his hope, he said, that these new facts might just shake loose the killer or someone with some tidbit of knowledge that might move the case from its long-stalled position.

Cynics would have told you that Bratcher's press conference was "just a gesture," as one reporter called it, "to deflect eyes from the deliberations of the Crime Commission and the BGA." Others believed, with a considerable show of optimism, that the new information might, indeed, break the blanket of silence that shrouded the case.

The task force now officially numbered only seven, including James Bell, who had been in charge for several months. After a career as an FBI major case specialist who studied serial killer Ted Bundy and coordinated investigations into dozens of major crimes, Bell retired and then, in March 1995, he was hired by the village of Palatine. Bratcher named him task force leader, hoping he would bring not only his expertise but a fresher perspective to the case.

This was Bell's second tour of duty with the force. When the group was initially assembled immediately after the murders, he had been part of a team dispatched by the FBI to Palatine. He had stayed for two weeks and then moved on. In the years before his retirement, he had continued his FBI job, flying around the country to meet with detectives similarly stymied.

Much of Bell's knowledge about serial killers and mass murderers came from interviews with more than a hundred investigators who had handled some of the biggest cases in the country. Over, the course of these interviews, he had developed a systematic method for examining and coordinating complicated cases that involved dozens of detectives and the processing of thousands of leads. After leaving the task force, he had stayed in contact with Palatine investigators, in part, he later said, because he understood the pressure the task force members felt. "Most of the pressure is put on them by themselves," he would later say. "I mean, it becomes your sole goal in life to solve that case."

Now Bell stood shoulder to shoulder with Bratcher as they unveiled select pieces of evidence in an attempt to jump-start the investigation. A considerable amount of the information they detailed had the feel of old news, thanks to various leaks and repeated speculations, and had already been taken as fact. There was just one shooter, they said. "We have a high level of confidence there is one killer," Bell said. Still, he conceded that they were not ruling out the possibility that the killer had had an accomplice.

"There was one meal purchased, there was one type of shoe print and one gun was used to kill all the victims," Bell said. Because the last receipt was timed by the cash register as 9:08 P.M., Bell said investigators believed the killer had paid for a meal just after closing to assure being alone with the employees.

Bell picked up a white shoe and held it up for reporters, who were busy scribbling in their notebooks. The shooter, he said, wore Nike Air Force brand athletic shoes, size twelve and a half to fourteen. This conclusion had been reached by examining shoe prints inside the restaurant in consultation with a Nike footwear expert. The print suggested the shoe was relatively new at the time the print was left and that it had been manufactured sometime between June 1990 and November 1992.

The task force had succeeded in keeping the shoe evidence quiet, and it had been particularly valuable as a tool to rule out suspects. If the evidence had been revealed, the killer might have disposed of the shoes. But now, after three years, the investigators reasoned that if they were still in existence, the shoes would be so worn down that making any comparisons based on the print marks found in the restaurant would be unreliable at best and likely impossible.

The shoe evidence had already proved its worth to the investigators because José Cruz, the subject of Lead 80, wore a size eight. For that reason alone, Bell and Bratcher reiterated, he was not the killer. Bratcher felt at this moment that it was important to repeat his view of Lead 80. "It's been beaten to death," he told the reporters. "It has no legs. It can't stand on its own."

The killer's height, Bell and Bratcher told reporters, was somewhere between six feet and six feet six inches, and he—there had never been any speculation that the killer might have been a female—used a .38- or .357- caliber revolver. The killer collected the expended shells and reloaded the gun several times. Mounted for display for reporters were four guns that could have fired the bullets that were recovered from the victims, including a black revolver with a six-inch barrel and a stainless-steel revolver with a snub-nosed barrel. This was a vivid indication of the fact that knowing the caliber of a weapon is only a small part of the equation and a reminder that there were no witnesses who saw the weapon used in the massacre.

Further, Bell said, investigators—based on interviews with people who were along the highway and near the Brown's parking lot about the time of the massacre— believed the killer had a car that resembled a late-1980s- model Camaro, most likely white in color.

Though some of these details were already known, some were tantalizing for members of the media, frustrated as they had been in their ability to pierce the wall of silence Bratcher and the task force had created. But as interesting as the disclosures were, Bratcher acknowledged that the case now seemed to depend not on what the investigators could decipher, but on someone with information deciding to contact authorities. "We said from the beginning that it might take one phone call, one critical phone call to solve this crime," he said. "It is our hope that this evidence will trigger the recollection of someone who may know the person responsible for this crime."

The media coverage of the press conference triggered

a barrage of telephone calls the following day. Palatine police commander James Haider told reporters that more than 120 people had called with tips, and that about sixty-five of those tips provided investigators with new leads. Some of them, he said, were intriguing. "We think this is a good showing," Haider said. "We're pleased."

It was a hopeful moment at a time when there seemed to be no hope. The men once considered top suspects were no longer viewed as viable possibilities. The theory of Cruz's involvement had been ridiculed and discarded. The next best suspects, Robert Faraci and Paul Modrowski, had finally gone to trial for the murder of Dean Fawcett in neighboring Barrington. Their cases had been decided simultaneously before separate juries. Almost inexplicably, Faraci, who admitted being in the field when the victim was shot and beheaded, was acquitted, while Modrowski, who admitted to nothing, was convicted and sentenced to life in prison. Modrowski, investigators believed, had nothing to do with the Brown's murders and Faraci contended he had an alibi for the night of the killings. Neither was considered seriously anymore by task force members, though Bratcher, somewhat mysteriously, said both men were still listed officially as suspects.

But at the same time that task force members were finally lowering their wall of silence, they were battling in court to keep other information secret. The Castro and Solis families' lawsuits against Brown's were still pending and lawyers for Portillo continued to contend that they needed the investigative files to properly defend against the charges of being negligent in providing security at the restaurant. The task force was still steadfastly arguing that the release of sensitive information could make the case more difficult, if not impossible, to solve.

Glen Sechen, an attorney for the village of Palatine, told the *National Law Journal* that task force members were concerned that disclosure would jeopardize any possible confession obtained from a suspect because it would leave police without information, known only to them, that they could use to weed out false confessors. "Disclosure of general facts is not the problem," Sechen said. "It's the publication of unique facts surrounding the crime that could ruin an otherwise valuable confession."

Despite the task force position, Cook County Circuit Court judge Michael Hogan ordered some of the files turned over for his private review and he then ordered some of them turned over to Portillo's lawyers. Hogan said he was balancing the interest of the task force in solving the murders against the interests of the Brown's chain. Hogan said he wanted to examine certain photographs of the crime scene and a cash register tape that showed the last sale. And Hogan said he also wanted to review police logs showing any calls made to police from restaurant employees in the three years before the murders—possible evidence that lawyers for the Solis and Castro families could use to show that the restaurant had had a history of trouble with customers, but that its owners had still made no effort to beef up security measures in response.

Hogan did toss one bone to the task force: He issued a protective order barring Portillo's lawyers from passing any of the documents or information along to the press. Still, investigators were concerned that information could be leaked, possibly unintentionally, and wind up in the media, prompting witnesses or informants to remain silent forever for fear of retribution from the killer. And disclosure might cause the killer to destroy existing evidence

The victims: (from left to right)
Michael Castro, Thomas Mennes,
Rico Solis, Marcus Nellsen,
Guadalupe Maldonado, Lynn Ehlenfeldt,
Richard Ehlenfeldt.

(Copyright AP/Wide World Photos)

An aerial view as the police remove the bodies from the restaurant. (Copyright Chicago Tribune Company)

Two days after the killings, the restaurant looks deceptively peaceful. (Copyright Chicago Tribune Company)

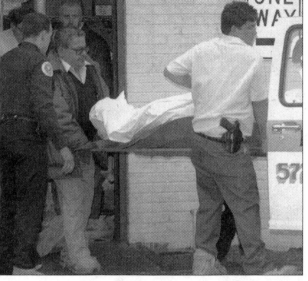

The police remove one of the bodies.

Roses line the ground outside the restaurant in remembrance of the seven people murdered there. (Copyright Chicago Tribune Company)

Investigators use metal detectors to search the restaurant parking lot for evidence. (Copyright Chicago Tribune Company)

Palatine Police Chief Jerry Bratcher at a press conference discussing the case. (Copyright Chicago Tribune Company)

Frank Portillo, President of Brown's Chicken and Pasta.

(Copyright Chicago Tribune Company)

Jane Homeyer, Northern Illinois Crime Lab technician who saved crucial evidence. (Copyright Chicago Tribune Company)

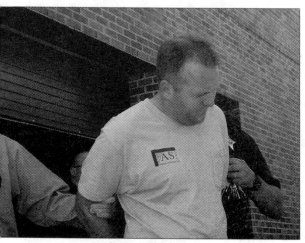

James Degorski being led away by Palatine police.

(Copyright Chicago Tribune Company)

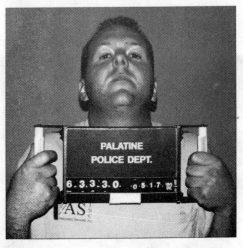

Juan A. Luna and James Eric Degorski after being charged with murdering seven people at a Brown's Chicken restaurant.

(Copyright Chicago Tribune Company)

that he might otherwise be unaware of or not have previously realized its significance.

Sechen also pointed out that there might be people who were accomplices or had learned information about the massacre through street gossip or perhaps even a relationship with the killer. Ominously, he added, "People who have killed seven others and are already eligible for the death penalty aren't going to be deterred by the death of one or two more."

TWENTY-ONE

UNSOLVED MURDERS ARE NO MORE UNUSUAL in Chicago than anywhere else. Since the 1920s, nearly eleven hundred murders have been attributed to Chicago's organized crime figures, but only one has resulted in the conviction of a mob hit man for murder. That case took two trials before Harry Aleman, a killer believed to be responsible for the murders of more than two dozen men, was found guilty in 1997 for a murder committed a quarter century before. Many of these unsolved beatings, stabbings, shootings, and stranglings have, over the years, taken on a mystique of their own—obtaining a sort of darkly romantic status because of the inability of law enforcement to solve them.

Former *Chicago Tribune* reporters John O'Brien and Ed Baumann wrote a book about such cases in 1991, entitled *Getting Away with Murder, 57 Unsolved Murders with Reward Information*. Their list of the most intriguing includes one of Chicago's highest-profile unsolved cases—that of Barbara and Patricia Grimes, two teenage sisters who went out to see an Elvis Presley movie in 1957 and were later found nude and murdered in a ditch. There are many other cases that continue to hold the public's interest—some new and some old. For example, in 1982, seven people died from taking Tylenol capsules laced with cyanide, and while one man was sent to prison for attempting to extort money from the makers of Tylenol, no one was convicted of the murders. Other cases include that of Benjamin Lewis, a Chicago alderman who was found shot four times in the back of the head in his office in 1963, and that of Judith Mae Anderson, a fifteen-year-old who disappeared while walking home from a friend's house and whose body was later found dismembered and stuffed in oil drums floating in Lake Michigan.

These are the sorts of cases that the media routinely resurrects on anniversaries of the murders in the way one takes out an old scrapbook or photo album in an attempt to rekindle memories. But in not one of these cases has an outside group ever attempted to intervene to conduct any sort of official review of whether the police had done their job correctly. But this was just what Brown's chain president Frank Portillo had asked the BGA and the Crime Commission to do.

In April 1996, more than three years after the Brown's massacre, Portillo got his wish when the Crime Commission and the BGA announced the formation of a ten-member panel to review the work of the Palatine Police Department and the task force. "In light of the many public and private allegations that the investigation was not thoroughly developed in Palatine, there appears to be a lack of public confidence in this major homicide investigation," said Donald Mulack, president of the Crime

Commission. "These allegations should be thoroughly examined by independent experts to restore public confidence in the investigation."

The panel would examine several issues: whether adequate resources and expertise were brought to the investigation in a timely manner; conflicting reports over the investigation of leads; the management of task force personnel; and whether a lack of cooperation among task force members had hindered the investigation.

The panel, Mulack said, would be chaired by James Osterburg, former head of the department of criminal justice at the American Academy of Forensic Science. Members of the panel included Joseph M. Brennan, a thirteen-year former FBI agent; Thomas P. Cawley, former supervising judge in the Cook County Circuit Court's criminal division; James T. McGuire, former superintendent of the Illinois State Police; Terrance A. Norton, former deputy chief of the organized crime section of the Department of Justice in Chicago; Michael E. Shabat, former first assistant Cook County state's attorney; Peter F. Vaira, a former U.S. attorney and executive director of the President's Commission on Organized Crime; Mary Dedinsky, associate dean and professor at Northwestern University's Medill School of Journalism and a former managing editor of the *Chicago Sun-Times;* H. Roderic Heard, a trial attorney and faculty member at DePaul University Law School; and Richard L. Thornburgh, former U.S. attorney general.

The panel would not attempt to solve the crime, Mulack said, but would initially focus on interviews with former members of the task force. All told, about one hundred twenty-five different investigators had been shuttled in and out of the task force—a group that now numbered only seven. He conceded that it was not clear, exactly, what impact any findings might have on the case. The report was expected to be completed within a year.

Mulack and J. Terrence Brunner, executive director of the BGA, reminded people that although Portillo had asked for the review, the final decision to go ahead had been made without his participation. Anticipating a negative reaction from Palatine police and the task force, Brunner urged investigators to cooperate. "This is a legitimate inquiry," he said.

Almost immediately, the review came under criticism.

"This body appears to be a shadow investigation," said Patrick O'Brien, who, as a Cook County assistant state's attorney, had formerly served on the task force. "We believe it would be very dangerous and potentially might prejudice or jeopardize the arrest and prosecution of the killer."

O'Brien said the panel was redundant because the task force had previously brought in outside, independent criminal justice experts to conduct a "cold-case review" of the investigation—a new revelation—and those experts had agreed that the task force and Palatine police had acted properly.

While investigators privately seethed at what they viewed as a thinly veiled attempt by Portillo to salvage his financially punished business and as meddling by the publicity-hungry BGA, O'Brien was diplomatic. "These are well-intentioned people," he said about the panel. "But this is an ill-advised concept. Our belief is that the authority and responsibility of law enforcement in an open case, a pending case, is to basically keep police reports and their files private and open only to other law enforcement agencies."

Within hours, a joint statement of support for the task force and the Palatine Police Department was issued by Cook County state's attorney Jack O'Malley, Chicago police superintendent Matt Rodriguez, Cook County sheriff Michael Sheahan, Illinois police superintendent Terrence Gainer, and Herbert Collins, chief of the Chicago division of the FBI. "Our offices have worked closely with the Palatine task force in its efforts to solve the brutal murders," the statement read. "We have the utmost confidence in the task force investigation."

Emil Mennes, the father of Brown's victim Thomas Mennes, would not say that the investigation had been botched. But still, since his concern was obtaining justice for his son, he thought a review might be worthwhile. "In a case like this, you never know if there's a mix-up or something," Mennes said. "It's good to have somebody checking it out."

Some critics of the BGA–Crime Commission collaboration pointed out that other review panels such as the Warren Commission, which reviewed the investigation of the assassination of President John F. Kennedy, and the Kerner Commission, which investigated riots that followed the assassination of Martin Luther King and during the Democratic presidential convention in Chicago in 1968, had accomplished little.

Edward Tromanhauser, chairman of the criminal justice department at Chicago State University, told the *Chicago Tribune* that all too frequently recommendations and conclusions from such reviews are either discounted or ignored. "Many of the criticisms and recommendations from those commissions were as valid today as when they were issued, and still, nothing has been done," he said. "I don't think very much of blue-ribbon panels in general."

Other critics, perhaps prompted by detectives who had worked on the case, were quick to remind people that the inspiration for the review had been Portillo, who was a defendant in the Castro and Solis lawsuits alleging that the company had failed to provide adequate security. But Portillo said that once he had requested that the two groups conduct the review, he was excluded from the decision-making process. "I have been completely out of the loop since I made the request for them to review the case," he said. "I couldn't even go to Crime Commission board meetings. I didn't know the panel had been formed or who was even picked out until the last minute."

He added, "I'm just a frustrated and angry citizen and businessman who feels the system is not working. How could my desire to solve this case affect the outcome of a lawsuit? All I want is for the various law enforcement agencies to work together harmoniously to affect a final resolution and let the chips fall where they may.

"We've got to be bigger than personalities," he went on. "We have an opportunity to show the citizens of Illinois that when two very prestigious watchdog organizations get together and are united without ego, we will find out if the government is working harmoniously on behalf of all the people."

But there was a very real question about whether the panel would be able to accomplish anything. Chief Bratcher, fuming internally, flatly said the police and task force would not cooperate in any way. There would be no interviews with task force members and no reports would be turned over. Still, he maintained a professional attitude. "These are people of integrity, so I'm not going to blast them," he said. "I don't know the mission that's been developed for them, but it's more than a little puzzling to me why these people would accept this if they knew the whole story."

The Palatine Village Board unanimously passed a resolution supporting the department and the task force. The resolutions said that the BGA and Crime Commission were "accountable to no one and . . . have no legal or procedural standing to investigate anything in Palatine and should immediately end this investigation." Further, village officials advised Bratcher against spending significant amounts of time cooperating with the panel.

Mike Lyons, chief investigator for the BGA, remained resolute. "We are not even the slightest bit concerned that the task force won't cooperate," he told the *Chicago Tribune*. "We've been doing investigations of government agencies for a long time. I have every confidence in our ability to obtain a substantial amount of information."

Whether he needed to or not, Brunner appeared to issue what many felt was a challenge or an outright insult to Bratcher and the task force when he said, "They must be terribly, terribly nervous to be this defensive."

TWENTY-TWO

T HE NEWS OUT OF NASHVILLE WAS GRUESOME, the sort of news that makes most people cringe and perhaps even say a prayer, thankful to be alive. It's possible some of the Palatine task force members were saying prayers of a different sort as they traveled to the Tennessee city in the spring of 1996 to learn more about a crime spree in which six people had been killed in three separate robberies of fast-food restaurants. "We would classify this as a very important lead at this point," task force leader James Bell told the *Chicago Tribune*. "What we have is two composites from different crime scenes, but the descriptions are very close."

The crimes were carried out in similar fashion: Workers were found fatally shot and their bodies left in the walk-in coolers. Two employees at a Captain D's restaurant were killed during a robbery on February 16. On March 23, three workers at a McDonald's restaurant were murdered in a late-night holdup. A fourth person at the McDonald's survived when the gunman missed with his last bullet and stabbed the victim before he fled. Not long afterward, one person was killed in a Shoney's restaurant.

In addition to the similarities in how the crimes occurred, police said the suspect was described as six feet two inches tall, which was within the range of height estimated for the killer in the Brown's massacre. Bell said that investigators were hoping that someone might recall seeing a "real, real big guy" near Brown's just before the murders. "What we're mostly interested in is anybody in the northern suburbs in Cook County who knows someone who is male, white, very big, in Palatine around January of 1993, and has since left, gone or passed through Nashville," Bell said.

The attacker was described as being a white male in his late twenties to midthirties with a thin to medium build, a mustache, and dark hair that was almost shoulder length.

Chief Bratcher said, "We're very, very interested in these murders. There are a lot of parallels. We're looking at it, yes. Is there a solid connection at this point? No."

But, Chicago police captain Tom Cronin, a criminal profiler, told the *Tribune* that he believed that the chance that the Nashville murders were linked to the Palatine case was "far removed—most remote. That's just not what serial killers do. The motivation behind serial killers is usually power, control or sexually oriented. Just because people are killed and put into a freezer, that's not unusual. People have been robbing food chains and putting people into freezers as long as we've had walk-in freezers because it gives the bad guy an easy way out."

Still, the task force hoped that someone would come

forward in response to an airing of the case—and comparisons to the Nashville murders—on the *America's Most Wanted* television program. A detective was dispatched from Palatine to the show's Washington, D.C., headquarters, where he sat with the show's crew of twenty-four operators, ready to personally take any calls that sounded especially promising. But nothing happened. There were no legitimate calls.

In June, Nashville detectives arrested thirty-nine-year-old Paul Dennis Reid Jr. and charged him with the McDonald's and Captain D's murders. Reid had been arrested at a Shoney's restaurant where he had recently been fired as a dishwasher after he attempted to kidnap a supervisor. Reid had been put in a lineup, and the survivor of the McDonald's attack identified him as the attacker. Police searched Reid's apartment and found more than $1,100 in change and a box of bloody gloves—evidence they believed linked him to both crimes. They did note that Reid was six feet three inches tall and wore a size-twelve shoe, again well within the range theorized for the Brown's killer.

Reid, a former resident of Richland Hills, Texas, was a bad man. He had previously been convicted of an aggravated armed robbery for shooting up a restaurant in Houston during a robbery. He had served seven years of a twenty-year prison sentence and had been released in January 1990. He had been placed on parole, and in 1993 had been allowed to modify the terms of the parole to require that he write his parole officer once a year or if he moved. Texas officials said Reid had complied with the requirements.

Task force investigators were in frequent contact with Nashville detectives. A set of Reid's fingerprints was sent to the Illinois State Police Crime Laboratory to compare to still-unidentified fingerprints that had been recovered from the Brown's restaurant. Authorities in Palatine and Nashville were restrained in their public comments. Nashville police chief Emmett Turner said that no connection to the Brown's massacre had been established. Bell said, "We're treating Reid just like every other person who comes to our attention. We're going through, being very methodical, and seeing whether he matches up to our case." Perhaps more significantly, he noted, "If anything had knocked this out, we wouldn't still be working on him."

Bell issued a plea to the public for help in establishing if Reid was in the Chicago area at the time of the Brown's massacre. Reid's photograph was published in newspapers and shown on television news broadcasts. Palatine police commander Jim Haider said, "The arrest of Mr. Reid is significant in these Nashville homicide cases because of the similarities to Brown's. We are asking anyone who knew or might have known Mr. Reid in Chicago to give us a call."

Parole officials in Texas said their records showed that Reid had been living in Ft. Worth and employed by a uniform company when the Brown's massacre occurred. He had been hurt in a work-related car accident in 1991, but because he was kept on the company payroll, he was able to tell his parole officer that he was employed. Parole officials conceded that Reid could have been anywhere. He had written his parole officer in February of that year and then again four months later when he moved to Oklahoma, where he held several jobs, most recently as a baker in a grocery store.

Nashville police said Reid had been fired from the Shoney's on February 15, 1996. The next day, a manager at the Captain D's, a fast-food fish chain owned by Shoney's, and a coworker were murdered and left in the walk-in cooler.

Reid was also considered a suspect in the April kidnapping and murder of two ice cream workers in Clarksville, Tennessee. A witness reported seeing a red car near the scene of the murders, and Reid, investigators said, had rented such a car in March. He also was reported to have a girlfriend in Clarksville.

The reports of Reid's arrest and the publication of his photograph triggered several telephone calls to the Brown's task force from people saying they might have seen him in the Chicago area about the time of the murders. One of the callers, a former rodeo rider and country singer named Chad McCarthy, told the *Chicago Sun-Times* that in late January or early February 1993, he saw a man who fit Reid's description several times in Dumas Walker's, a tavern in Mt. Prospect, a suburb near Palatine. McCarthy said he knew the man as Paul Rogers. "I spit my tea across the room when I saw him on television," McCarthy said. "I know he is the one I saw." McCarthy said he talked to Palatine detectives about the sighting and recalled that Reid had said he was just passing through. "I didn't ask him more than that," McCarthy told the *Sun-Times*.

A bartender at the tavern also called the task force after seeing a photograph of Reid in the newspaper. Rox Stuker told the *Sun-Times* that Reid looked like a former customer and she asked the task force if she could see more pictures. "He looks like a guy who used to come in here," she said. "That's why I wanted to see other pictures of him. I'm pretty good at remembering names and faces."

But Dorothy Meadlin, Reid's former landlord in Ft. Worth, insisted that from 1991 to 1993, when he rented an apartment from her, he never traveled to Chicago. She said he was "absolutely not in Chicago in January of 1993. The only time he traveled was to see his family at Christmas and he left the day before and came back the day after," she said.

Meadlin said that Reid had spent the first three months of 1993 undergoing a series of operations that required him to stay at home. Reid had paid for the operations with a $25,000 workers' compensation award he had received after a job injury. "In January of 1993 he was here having his face peeled, his teeth straightened and his ears pinned back," Meadlin told the *Ft. Worth Star Telegram*. "He'd come into some money and said he had acne that had left scars and it was something he always wanted to do." She said he moved out of the apartment in April of that year.

From his jail cell, Reid told a reporter for the *Nashville Tennessean* that he had never been to Palatine in his life. "Why would I go there in the wintertime, being a Texan who don't know how to drive in the snow?" he said.

Reid's arrest compelled members of the media to make yet another round of telephone calls to family members of the Brown's victims, asking the same questions: Have you heard about the latest possible suspect? How do you feel? Are you hopeful?

Jennifer Ehlenfeldt told the *Tribune* that the time when the midnight telephone call would trigger a river of memories and a flood of hope that perhaps this would be the one had long passed. "I used to be so hopeful," she said. "But I'm not like that anymore. I've moved on. I don't let it dominate my life anymore.

"You kind of have to guard yourself against being too

optimistic," Ehlenfeldt said. "Sure, this might provide closure in some ways. But to some of us, we'll never have closure."

Emil Mennes, whose son, Thomas, was among the murder victims, had a similar response. "I used to get my hopes up, but I don't have much hope anymore," he said. "I don't see the point." After the death of his wife, Frances, in 1995, Mennes realized that that hope had been one of their great bonds. Now, he said, he found himself feeling almost indifferent. "I guess I'm still interested," he said. "I don't know."

Jennifer Ehlenfeldt said that at each year's anniversary of the crime, or on days when the case moved back to the front page of the newspapers because of a possible suspect, she tried to focus on happier times rather than the murders. "I remember the good things," she said. "It's always going to be there, the anniversary. I just try to get through the day."

Vela Urgena, Rico Solis's grandmother, was equally matter-of-fact. "We just aren't going to be focusing on this until there is actually someone arrested," she said. "There's no point to it. Why go through it emotionally if this turns out to be nothing?"

And that's what it did turn out to be. Before June was out, a dermatologist in Dallas provided documentation to police showing that Reid had made his first visit at 2:45 P.M. on January 8, 1993. The Brown's massacre occurred more than nine hundred miles away and sometime after 9 P.M. on that night. While Palatine police declined to rule Reid out—they continued to refer to him as an "interesting person"—it was clear that he was not the killer they were seeking.

TWENTY-THREE

As FAR AS SNAPPY TITLES GO, THE ONE AT-tached to the better government association report was almost incendiary: "Patent Malarkey: Public Dishonesty and Deception."

In November 1997, almost eighteen months after undertaking the mission, the BGA issued a report on the Palatine Police Department and the task force investigation of the Brown's massacre. It was a blistering broadside that ripped the investigation for a long list of sins.

"Although no doubt sincere in its desire to solve the crime, the Palatine Police force was inexperienced in major homicide investigations," the report concluded. "Yet, after the task force was assembled, Palatine officers, rather than more experienced officers who then became available, still remained in key positions of responsibility on the task force."

But this conclusion was greeted with less-than-unanimous agreement. The panel of experts that had been assembled by the BGA and the Chicago Crime Commission issued a separate report of the investigation, one that contained many of the same criticisms but was far more measured in its language. It was not given a catchy title, but instead was labeled "Report of the Panel."

How two separate reports came to be written was not immediately clear. But many observers felt it fair to assume that one of two things had happened. Either the BGA issued its own separate analysis because its members believed the expert panel did not intend to go far enough in its criticism of the task force, or the expert panel chose to issue its own report to distance itself from the shrill tone of the BGA report.

By any account, even the expert panel's report offered a harsh assessment. It characterized the Palatine police officers as "overwhelmed by the magnitude of the case" and criticized them roundly for several major missteps. These failures included not taking seriously the missing person reports made by family members of the victims; not conducting a thorough and timely canvassing of the neighborhood around the restaurant; inadequately securing the crime scene, which resulted in the contamination and destruction of evidence; inept coordination of more experienced investigative personnel; not integrating a variety of resources that were available from the wide range of law enforcement agencies who were members of the task force; and poor communication between the command and the rank and file within the task force.

All of this, the expert panel's report claimed, contributed to a delayed discovery of the crime scene and "three wasted days of investigative efforts" pursuing early suspect Martin Blake while "ignoring all other investigative avenues."

The lapses, the expert panel's report said, may have been critical. One member of that panel noted that had a more thorough canvassing been conducted immediately, police would have learned that a twenty-four-hour gas station located nearby had a security video camera that might have caught the killers on tape before or after the murders. But the camera was not discovered until two weeks later, and by that time the videotape from the night of the killings had been erased.

The Cook County State's Attorney's Office, the expert panel's report stated, "departed from its traditional role, which is to allow the police to solve the crime, and instead insinuated itself into a murder investigation and ultimately emerged as a leader of the task force." As a result, state's attorney's investigative personnel who were inexperienced in major homicide investigations wound up in key tactical command positions, the report said.

At a joint news conference, where the findings of both the BGA and the expert panel were disclosed for the media, the BGA's Terrence Brunner and members of the expert panel did agree on one major point. Both called for the formation of a regional police team that would be trained to solve major crimes. Such a team would lead investigations instead of leaving them to local police chiefs with little experience.

And both reports also said the failure to share critical investigative information among the task force members had resulted in internal disputes that led to the "inappropriate release" of José Cruz, then considered a prime suspect. These internal disputes undermined many task force members' confidence in its leadership and led to feuding among experienced investigators from the various agencies. Ultimately, the task force had become ineffective, the two reports found.

"How many dead bodies have to pile up before somebody says we've got to be prepared?" said Crime Commission president Thomas Kirkpatrick. "Even the best system can be screwed up by bad people, and even the best people can be screwed up by a bad system. We want everyone to be able to give it their best shot—to make it possible for good people to get things done in a good system."

But beyond that, Kirkpatrick also made it clear that the BGA report was separate and distinct from that of the expert panel. "They're not our findings; they're the BGA's findings," he said.

Even with the title set aside, the BGA report was far more strident than that of the expert panel and it was peppered with vitriol. It said that task force mistakes "led quickly to a defensive posture with the media and the public." As a result, more emphasis was placed on creating positive public relations "spin" than on forming an effective law enforcement team. The BGA report said that the department had publicly taken positions "often contradicted by the facts available to the task force."

The BGA report further asserted that Palatine police officers with little or no experience had run the investigation in the beginning and later took positions of authority in the task force. One officer had been working as a high-school liaison officer, it said, and another investigator's homicide experience consisted of being on a surveillance detail in one case and taking some classes in homicide investigation.

The *Chicago Tribune,* quoting an unnamed suburban police chief, reported, "People say Palatine was a task force; it wasn't. It came after the fact. It was bodies thrown together, not working as a team to solve this. Imagine if you had this same team, but that it had trained together for two or three years. I think you'd see a difference."

A source close to the review who was not named told the *Tribune* that while the average suburban police department has 40 officers, the range went from just a few to as many as 150. In a department of 40 members, about 10 officers are on duty at any given time, the source said. "The question is, 'How many of the 10 know what to do with a big homicide case?' The answer isn't encouraging."

The BGA report didn't stop there. In agonizing detail, it attacked Bratcher as "a manipulative, incompetent 'feudal' leader." The *Chicago Sun-Times* described the department as made up of "Barney Fife-like neophytes." The BGA report noted that while the lack of murders in Palatine before the Brown's massacre was not unusual for a suburban police force, such low numbers meant investigators didn't have a great deal of homicide experience. "Bratcher's troops were like the Argentine Army—generals with chests full of medals who had never seen combat and suddenly, the Falklands, and it all began to crumble against the battle-tested British," the BGA report said.

It seemed like Bratcher, the BGA report said, "had it made." He was earning $80,000 a year as chief, had set up a consulting business that analyzed other suburban police departments, and was a consultant for a business that was owned by village trustees (who, the report said, ran the village police and fire committee). That business sold supplies to other suburban police departments. The firm that retained him as a consultant had handled the cleanup at the Brown's restaurant after the murders—at no charge, company officials said.

Combined with what the report termed Bratcher's "strong personal relationship" with Mayor Mullins, the result was that any real overseeing of the police department by the village government was "compromised."

"Bratcher's kingdom rested on a fragile foundation," the BGA report said. "Because the success of his outside interests rested upon good relationships with other suburban police chiefs, Bratcher had to constantly stroke them while at the same time hiding from them the true nature and extent of his business dealings and how they might affect the other chiefs.

"He became a prisoner of his own propaganda," the BGA report went on to claim. "He had to constantly exaggerate and puff his own accomplishments and those of his police force to keep his outside business interests rolling."

The BGA report was remarkable for the intensity of its attack on Bratcher. It said he attended "informal gettogethers" at a restaurant that was "a hangout for members of the law enforcement community" and "spent many hours in its bar." One unnamed police chief was quoted as saying, "We'll go in at noon and we'll still be in there at 8:00 p.m." Another chief was quoted as saying that a designated driver was discussed at these gatherings "in anticipation of the large amount of alcohol that would be consumed." Further, the BGA report said, members of the Palatine task force drank and dined at these gatherings on numerous occasions.

The report didn't just single out Bratcher, either. Cook County state's attorney Jack O'Malley was described as

a publicity-seeking, ambitious man whose main agenda
during the months after the massacre was cementing his
political future with an eye at a run for governor of Illinois. Those plans had been derailed in the fall of 1996
when O'Malley lost his bid for a third term as state's
attorney. O'Malley's press aide, Andy Knott, was quoted
in the BGA report as saying, "He's never met a micro-
phone he didn't like." O'Malley, the report charged, had
muscled into the task force because he thought the case
would be solved quickly and that he could take part of
the credit.

The Northern Illinois Police Crime Laboratory did not
escape criticism, either. The lab, the BGA report concluded, had failed to assign a top priority to processing
crime scene evidence and was hamstrung by a shortage
of experienced analysts. The report quoted an unnamed
former lab employee as saying, "I have witnessed poor
quality work being performed, incorrect reports being sent
out, and analysts working outside their area of expertise."

Another unnamed lab worker was quoted as saying that
at the time of the Brown's massacre, several analysts
spent more energy focusing on an analysis of "bird feces"
found on cars in the northern suburbs than on the murders.
The BGA report also cited an article published in the
Daily Herald a month after the killings that said evidence
analysis was taking too long. "Law enforcement sources
say the delay is primarily due to the Palatine Task Force's
almost total reliance for evidence processing on a north
suburban crime lab . . . and the crime lab's minimal use
of help offered by a more experienced crime lab run by
Chicago and the State Police," the article had reported.

One particular instance stood out, the BGA report said,
as "bizarre and inexplicable." During the first three weeks

after the murders, the task force "steadfastly refused to give sample bullets to the Chicago Police Crime Laboratory despite the fact that the Chicago lab had access to many thousands of weapons confiscated from Chicago streets every year."

"They weren't interested in our help at the time," Chicago lab personnel told the BGA. At the urging of a Chicago police detective, the task force relented, the BGA report said, and sent several bullets for analysis. But then the task force demanded them back in February. Curiously, the task force sent them back to the Chicago lab in May, but withheld one of the best samples, the report said, and "three months after the killings, all the Palatine evidence had not been processed." Part of the delay was the fault of the Palatine Police Department for holding on to some of the victims' clothing instead of sending it immediately to the lab.

Further, weeks after the killings and after obtaining ninety fingerprints from the crime scene, the lab had still not processed a single one, the BGA report said. In fact, one of the victims had not even been fingerprinted—a serious lapse because without those prints, others belonging to that individual could not be eliminated from the prints that remained unidentified. "Similarly, at least 17 vendors and former employees who had access to the front and rear areas of the restaurant in the days before the murders were neither questioned nor fingerprinted. Likewise, some Brown's employees were not fingerprinted until two-and-a-half years after the murders."

The BGA report quoted the February 1993 article in the *Daily Southtown Economist,* which said the lab was well behind in processing fingerprints because it refused to get help from other labs, such as the Chicago police lab. That was the report that Bratcher had branded "patent malarkey"—a phrase the BGA now used to mock him. At the time the article appeared, Bratcher had said the analysis was taking longer because more complex procedures were being employed. "It may not be as big as others, but it's staffed by professional people and they're doing it right," he said.

Of that statement, the BGA report said: "This was one of the most outrageous examples of the chief's deliberate misleading of the media and the public."

The actual processing of the crime scene was botched as well, the report contended. "Multiple sources told the BGA that approximately . . . 50 people trudged through the scene in addition to six unneeded paramedics. Tours were given. One eyewitness described the resulting crime scene as incredibly dirty, rendering virtually useless the papers that had been put down to cover the floor and protect possible evidence. As one person present at the scene commented, 'I'd call it a mess.' "

So many people went through the restaurant during the processing that a chart was prepared that contained their names and fingerprints for elimination purposes. The list included personnel from the police department's communication center, but not some of the police who were at the scene, the BGA report said.

Accompanying the BGA report was a statement from J. Terrence Brunner, its executive director. "Citizens have the right to know if their police department has the ability to handle a crime of this magnitude and, if they don't, do they have a plan to put into effect if one occurs?" the statement said. "The case of Palatine, however, proved to be especially unique. It had long been rumored there were internal problems on the task force but we were still surprised by the complexity of what was uncovered. We found that the spiderweb of cronyism and extra curricular economic interests, which existed both in the board of trustees and within the Palatine police department, influenced the most crucial decisions of the investigation and grossly undermined the village officials' authority, much less duty, to hold the chief accountable."

Experienced in the ways of public relations and sound bites and a polished self-promoter, the white-haired but still boyish-looking Brunner anticipated criticism in his statement. It was a masterpiece of egotistical, chest-thumping bravado, a preemptive strike, so to speak. "We routinely come under fire for these investigations and, as expected, the village of Palatine's response has been no exception," the statement said. "Those being exposed have always questioned the BGA's motivation. But our motive has always been to expose government corruption, fraud and waste and in that effort we go the extra distance. We are a citizens' watchdog group. We expose the truth. That's what we do."

At the news conference, Brunner quoted an unnamed woman who worked at the lab as saying the case would "never be solved on a scientific basis and the only way [it could be] is if someone comes forward and they can check his story against the facts." Brunner added, "I think she's probably pretty accurate."

The BGA had interviewed Portillo for its report, and his assessment of the investigation was equally severe. For instance, he had never been formally interviewed by the task force, the report said, and it was not until January 1996, three years after the murders, that the task force wrote to him to obtain a list of all vendors and workers at the restaurant prior to the massacre. Portillo had turned over a copy of the letter to the BGA investigators. "We were not aware that you had the information," the letter said.

According to the BGA report, the task force never analyzed the rare cottonseed oil used in the chicken's special recipe. "This cooking oil coated almost the entire restaurant, making it impossible for anyone in the restaurant to not have traces of the oil on their clothing, shoes and personal belongs. This oil could have conceivably been transferred to a getaway car by the killer(s). But police never checked evidence for the presence of cottonseed oil." Further, someone had spilled some of the oil on the floor during the processing of the crime scene, perhaps destroying or contaminating other evidence.

In particular, the BGA report blamed the state's attorney's office for bungling the investigation of Lead 80. The BGA took the side of Chicago homicide detective Richard Zuley, the detective who perhaps had been the most zealous pursuer of the theory that José Cruz and the Puerto Rican Stones street gang were responsible for the murders. In a long dissection of the investigation of Cruz, it noted that even after Zuley had been dismissed from the task force, he had continued to investigate Lead 80. Chicago Police Gang Crimes investigators had learned that Emmanuel Castro, whose son, Michael, was among the murder victims, had been arrested in May 1992, seven months before the slayings, for failure to exhibit a firearm registration certificate at his gun store. Further, Cruz, during his interrogation, had provided an accurate physical description of the elder Castro. That development had prompted investigators to suspect that Emmanuel Castro was selling guns to members of the Puerto Rican Stones gang. "Had Cruz known Manny Castro's son who was murdered at Brown's?" the BGA report asked, adding that for pushing that lead, even after he had been told to stay away from the Palatine investigation, Zuley had been given a one-day suspension.

"Current intelligence continues to implicate José Cruz and his gang in the Brown's Chicken massacre," the report said. It added that Chicago Police Gang Crimes detectives continued to receive leads, tips, and other intelligence almost weekly saying the massacre had been carried out by the Puerto Rican Stones street gang, but because the task force was not interested, these leads were no longer forwarded.

"The task force," the BGA report concluded, "effectively cut off the best source of intelligence in Illinois."

TWENTY-FOUR

A S ALMOST EVERYONE EXPECTED, THE RE-sponse to the BGA report was swift, angry, and forceful. Chief Bratcher called a news conference at the Palatine police station and opened it with a certain visual flair, holding up photocopies of the fingerprint cards of the seven murder victims.

"I can assure you," he said, "that these are all copies of the originals that reside at the Illinois crime lab." He said that all the victims had been printed at the Cook County Medical Examiner's Office soon after the murders. And he told the press that if that information was wrong in the BGA report, one had to wonder what else was incorrect.

"A reasonable, thinking person should pause to reflect on the diatribe emanating from the BGA," Bratcher said. No one present doubted that internally, Bratcher was furious—particularly at the personal nature of the report—but he relied upon the self-control honed in the U.S. Marine Corps and his more than a quarter century of police work to present a measured and calm demeanor.

Separately, Palatine mayor Rita Mullins called upon the Illinois State Crime Commission, another nonprofit private group, to investigate the BGA report and the expert panel's report as well. Almost immediately, officials in the ISCC agreed to assemble a panel to analyze the reports to determine if any of the accusations had merit, and to assess whether the recommendations were sound and necessary.

In a two-page statement, Mullins said, "For over a year, the public has been inundated with innuendo, leaks, and misinformation regarding the Brown's investigation. I am deeply concerned and displeased with the negative tone of the reports." She added, "It has not appeared to me, or the Palatine Village Council, that there has been a balanced assessment of the work performed by the Brown's task force."

Mullins accused the BGA and the expert panel of releasing their reports during local television stations' November rating sweeps period, one of the four months during which ratings dictate the amount stations can charge advertisers and which traditionally feature news broadcasts filled with titillating stories and controversial topics. "I think this is a fairy tale, this novelette they have put together," she said. "I think when the feeding frenzy is over, there's going to be no story. It is conjecture, supposition."

Although the BGA said more than a hundred interviews had been conducted, it claimed that it had been hamstrung by the refusal of Bratcher and the task force to provide any documentation, because, they believed, to do so would have jeopardized an ongoing criminal inquiry.

Bratcher took issue with the BGA's finding that more than fifty people went through the crime scene and contaminated evidence. "That's blown way the hell out of proportion," he said at his press conference. He said the people at the crime scene included investigators who went past the perimeter outside the restaurant but never actually went inside. He declined to respond to questions from the media about just how many people had been inside the restaurant.

In the days following the release of the reports, the conversation between the principals, as it was being conducted in the press, began to resemble the childish taunts of playground rivals, with the BGA's Brunner doing most of the talking. He scoffed at Bratcher's assertions by saying, "I think the guy would give you the hard sell that the sun rises in the West."

Bratcher unloaded to a *Daily Herald* reporter, saying, "Their findings are based on misinformation, innuendo, hearsay, half-truths and outright lies. To me, this examination into our investigation has not been a legitimate investigation, it's been an inquisition."

Brunner told the *Tribune*, "We have just as much right as anybody to look at this. The little old lady in tennis shoes who goes to every village board meeting has a right to look at this."

Frank Portillo defended the BGA and the Crime Commission for conducting an investigation, saying, "Any citizens' organization has the right to question a government official in America."

"It's a Salem witch hunt," Mullins fired back. She specifically addressed the BGA's attack on Bratcher in an interview with *Herald* political editor Madeleine Doubek. "This is a person I have worked with for 17 years," she said, referring to Bratcher. "I don't know what they mean by a personal relationship. It's somebody I have known. I don't go to his house; he doesn't come to my house. I see him at functions. I mean, what is the innuendo supposed to mean there?"

Asked to describe her relationship with Bratcher, Mullins said, "Just like the professional, working relationship that I have with, well, probably most of the department heads and probably two dozen employees because over the years you work together, you get to know people. It's just people you work with. There's some you get to be friends with and other people you say 'Hi' to in the hallway."

Mullins insisted that Bratcher's relationship with her and the village trustees had not damaged the investigation of the massacre. "Not one iota," she said. "It has nothing to do with anything. Everyone that works here in the village of Palatine are professional people. Our chief has been recognized nationally as a leader in his field and is a former Marine that put together the best task force that the FBI—I asked them myself and they said it was the best task force that they had ever seen.

"In fact," Mullins added, "they were going to replicate it—use it as a model for any other horrific crimes, God forbid, that would happen in the United States."

Then she took a shot at Brunner: "Is Brunner more of an expert than the guy from the FBI whose job it is to go in and help with these major crimes?"

Jane Homeyer, the evidence analyst from the Northern Illinois Police Crime Laboratory who had found the remains of a chicken meal in a clean garbage bag and or-

dered it preserved for future testing, was by this time the
executive director of the lab. She fired back at the BGA
report's accusation that lab work in the case took too long
to complete. She said that the lengthy processing time was
the result of technicians' carefulness in carrying out their
analyses. "From a crime lab standpoint, you want to be
thorough so mistakes don't happen," she told the *Chicago
Sun-Times*.

Bratcher said, "It's been very difficult from the beginning. They've been sniping at us from the weeds . . . and
sometimes we can't comment because it is sensitive to the
investigation. I'm confident that if half of what these people allege is true, I would have been gone four years
ago—if half of it was true, I *should* have been gone four
years ago."

While acknowledging that some police chiefs in surrounding suburbs were starting to believe that the case
would never be solved, Bratcher said he still felt the killer
or killers would eventually be identified and arrested. "I
have to cling to that," he told the *Herald*. "Clearly, the
more time that goes by, the fainter it gets. We're hopeful
something will break."

While Bratcher defended the work of the Brown's task
force, he conceded that the idea of a standing task force
had merit. "The formation of our task force worked very
well for us in the Brown's case," he said. "But when you
have a team of investigators that has trained and worked
together as a team, that will make a positive difference."

Lake County, directly north of Cook County, had already put such a task force in place, as had nearby DuPage
and McHenry Counties. The formation of task forces in
the northwest and south suburbs of Cook County were
already under discussion. Several northwest suburban po-

lice departments, including Palatine, had joined together to create a unit called the Major Case Assistance Team and assigned some thirty detectives to begin training. The unit was expected to help local police departments investigate—and solve—murders, rapes, and crimes involving arson.

While he supported the formation of this unit, Bratcher said that he could not imagine that it would ever, without outside assistance, be able to handle crimes the magnitude of the Brown's massacre. "I don't know of any other suburban department that has experienced anything on the order of Brown's and I hope to goodness no one has to," he said. "But we recognized in the Brown's case that you have to rely on other agencies for assistance, and that's what we did."

Portillo said he was hopeful that the reports would result in better coordination of murder investigations. "As much as I'd love to find the killers and dig a big hole in the ground and put them in it, I think it's changing the system that's more important," he told the *Tribune*.

Family members of the victims, whose telephones started to ring whenever the case returned to the front page or the top of the television and radio broadcasts, were reluctant to criticize the task force, despite the BGA findings. Diane Clayton, mother of victim Marcus Nellsen, told the *Herald* that the BGA report was not "concrete proof" of bungling. "You have to hold onto your hope," she said. "Without believing in the police department, I have no hope that it will be solved."

Larry Mennes, brother of victim Thomas Mennes, said he doubted that the case would ever be solved, but backed up the police work that had been done on it. "I think the Palatine Police Department has probably done everything it could have done," he said. And then he echoed what many people, among them some of the area's most seasoned and cynical reporters, were thinking, "This report itself sounds so political to me."

TWENTY-FIVE

A DECADE AFTER THE BROWN'S MASSACRE, JERRY Bratcher found himself still living in Palatine. Many who saw him found it difficult to imagine that he had retired as chief of police in 1999. Though retired, he remained in close touch with many of the officers he once commanded and so passionately defended from criticism over how the investigation was handled.

His life as chief came to an end in August 1999, after thirty-nine years in law enforcement and the last quarter of a century as chief of Palatine police. He did so with only one regret: his failure to break the Brown's case.

"I was consumed by it for the first two or three years," he told the *Chicago Tribune*'s Eric Ferkenhoff in a story that ran on August 15, two days after his retirement. "As time passes, it lightens some, but it hasn't gone away. It won't go away. It will still be on my mind, part of me forever, I guess. That it wasn't successfully brought to a conclusion by the time I left, it's been with me. It's al-

ways been with me and always will be with me. But at
the same time, I make no apologies."

Bratcher could have retired two years earlier, but
stayed on as the village lost several veteran administrators
and new officials were becoming familiar with their jobs.
After he retired, Deputy Chief Jack McGregor was named
permanently to the chief's job.

One village official remarked that the case had taken a
physical toll on Bratcher, cracking his Marine drill sergeant exterior. "You could tell and feel and you could see
that he was feeling really, really sad for the families," Jack
Wagner, chairman of the village public safety commission, told the *Daily Herald*. Wagner, who had worked
closely with Bratcher, said, "I think the police department
did every single thing they could to bring that thing to
closure. I think it bothers him personally that whoever did
this so far has gotten away with it. But I still think that
in the back of his mind, he believes it will be solved one
day."

Bratcher said he would willingly trade all his honors
to have the case solved. "I hate to see the stigma on Palatine, but as far as I'm personally concerned, I'm a professional police administrator. It happened on my watch,
and if there's criticism to come down, it should land on
my shoulders. And it has. If they want to take a shot, they
should shoot at me," he said.

In a way, he was not really leaving. The village had
hired him back as a part-time consultant for $20,000 a
year to help identify and hire personnel for key village
departments. Still, many honors and much praise were be-
stowed on him, and Bratcher seemed almost embarrassed
by it all. He and his wife planned to enjoy more time with
their son—an officer in the Palatine Police Department—

and their two daughters. And they intended to vacation more. When he left the department, he retired with a pension equal to half of his $106,700 salary. And the village purchased back his unused sick days for $32,400, a testament to Bratcher's work ethic since the village paid just $.45 cents on the dollar.

"Jerry Bratcher is one of the finest police chiefs who ever sat in the job," said Cook County Circuit Court judge Sam Amirante, who had known him for nearly a decade. "He's knowledgeable about the law. He studies. That type of knowledge filters down through his department."

Good Housekeeping magazine had named the Palatine Police Department among the top eight departments in the nation in 1996. Under Bratcher, Palatine's force was one of the first in the nation to receive accreditation from the Commission on Accreditation for Law Enforcement Agencies. Bratcher later served on the commission and received national recognition for his work on police accreditation standards. He also developed the "dual ladder" concept, which rewards not just seniority but also expertise. Palatine was also the first department in Illinois to begin a Drug Abuse Resistance Education program, aimed at discouraging drug use and targeting children at an early age. And Palatine was the first department in Illinois to require entry-level officers to have a bachelor's degree.

At the time of Bratcher's retirement, Palatine police commander Brad Grossman compared the chief's relationship with members of the force to that of a father and his sons. "A lot of us are feeling indebted to him for letting us have a career here," Grossman said.

Mundelein police chief Raymond Rose told the *Herald:* "Since the time Chief Bratcher has come into the northwest suburbs, he has used his skills as a foundation to build modern-day, non-traditional law enforcement techniques. He's viewed as a professional on the cutting edge." Rose also said: "He was a very progressive thinker and a visionary."

Bratcher was humbled by all the praise. "Sometimes they throw accolades at you at the end of a career," he said. "If anyone achieved anything, including me, it's because of the people around here. You don't work in a vacuum. I've been blessed." But still, he had regrets over his inability to solve the Brown's massacre. "My biggest is that I'm leaving with this unsolved," he said. "It looms large in my mind."

It certainly shared space there with memories of the many false hopes that had haunted the massacre. Just one year earlier, he and investigators had their hopes yet again raised when an Illinois man who had moved to Colorado admitted to task force members that he had been inside the Brown's restaurant on the night of the killings. Police had been given the man's name right after the killings and they were told he was in the restaurant that night. The man was not identified to the media at that time, but authorities in 1998 detailed his story.

They said that the man, a Palatine resident, had stated during his initial interview that he was not in the restaurant. During a review of the case in 1998, investigators— the task force was now down to just two full-time detectives and several part-timers—had decided to begin reinterviewing several individuals. So they had sat down with the man again. This time he acknowledged not only that he was in the restaurant, but that he might have been the last customer served before it closed. One source told the *Tribune*, "Somebody saw something that hadn't been checked before. So he was re-interviewed, and that's when his story changed. He now puts himself inside the restaurant."

The man's fingerprints had been sent to the Illinois State Police Crime Lab for comparison to more than a hundred others recovered from the restaurant. The process had taken several hundred hours. But to the disappointment, if not the surprise, of many, no match had been found.

After more than six years, the case had taken its toll not only on Bratcher, but on the families of the victims, on the residents who had lived in fear, and on the many investigators who had worked unstintingly for many, many hours. Task force leader James Bell said the investigators, though scaled back in number, still took their work seriously. "Anyone that comes across our line of vision is looked at," he told the *Herald*. "No one is eliminated unless we know where they were the night of the murders."

He estimated that about five hundred leads came in each year and each one was logged into a computer. "The computer tracks single leads," Bell said. "One lead may require 50 or 60 interviews or lab work before it's closed. If you were to stack up the paperwork, it would be the same as an eight-story building." A Web site created two years earlier had resulted in only ten leads, all of them fruitless—most tips still came through the telephone. "Sometimes people contact us with a hidden motive," Bell said. "It's a guy mad at another guy. Or a woman angry at her boyfriend."

And meanwhile, many of the subplots were playing out on different stages.

The lawsuit brought by the parents of Michael Castro and Rico Solis, accusing Brown's of failing to maintain

adequate security, had been tossed out of court. Lawyers
for the two families had vowed to appeal, but legal experts
predicted the case would never be reinstated. And they
were correct.

The site of the restaurant came back into the news
when Signature Cleaners, the dry-cleaning business that
tried to make a go of it in the building that had housed
Brown's, bailed out. After nearly four years in the space,
the owners said the 2,500-square-foot building was just
too large for their needs. The following month, July 1998,
Vincent V. Fiduccia Sr. and his son, Vincent Jr., unveiled
plans to open an upscale deli in the building, and though
the pair did begin renovating the space, work stalled and
eventually the Fiduccias backed out of the deal.

One of the reasons why they did so, perhaps, was that
Joy McClain, the fiancée of murder victim Marcus Nellsen, had begun a petition drive to have the Brown's restaurant site leveled and a memorial erected. Diane
Mennes, whose brother-in-law, Thomas Mennes, was
murdered as well, had joined her. "We don't want anything going in there, out of respect for those who were
killed," she had told the *Tribune*. Jerry Mennes, brother
of the victim, had a simpler thought: "They can have the
building. But I want a plaque to commemorate the people
that were killed there. They died earning a living."

Three months and seven hundred signatures later,
McClain abruptly changed her mind. "Now I look at the
building and I just don't see Brown's anymore," she told
the *Herald*. Indeed, the exterior renovations for the deli
had removed the wooden overhang that distinguished
many of the Brown's restaurants. She said she was still
reminded of the horror when news about the case
prompted the media to resurrect footage and photographs,

taking her and others back to January 9, 1993, in the snowy parking lot surrounded by yellow evidence tape as body bags were carried out to waiting ambulances.

But she still wanted the village to create some kind of memorial. "I know the victims were just average John Q. Citizens, but something should be done," she said. "A sculpture would be suitable. I've decided that's where I want to go with things."

One person with no more decisions to make or comments to give was Emil Mennes, Thomas Mennes's father. Two days after Bratcher's retirement, chief McGregor handled his first murder case in his new position when the seventy-six-year-old Mennes was found murdered in his condominium. He had been stabbed repeatedly in his chest and throat.

Within two weeks, a sixteen-year-old street gang member who lived in the same building turned himself in to police and confessed to the crime. He had killed Mennes, he said, because of the way the elderly man had looked at him in the hallway of the building. Melvin Paige admitted to being so enraged by that encounter that he had gone back to Mennes's unlocked apartment and waited until he returned, then attacked and killed him. The expression on Mennes's face, it turned out, had been the result of a stroke. Paige's confession provided a bit of odd comfort, for before it came, fear was rapidly spreading across the suburb. Members of the Mennes family and so many others almost instinctively associated any violent act in Palatine with the massacre, ever searching for links, wondering if the person or persons responsible for the massacre were somehow connected to other crimes. As McGregor put it: "I suppose this will remind people of the situation that occurred with Brown's. It reopens old wounds."

TWENTY-SIX

PERHAPS IT HAD SOMETHING TO DO WITH THE dawn of a new century, but for surprising reasons, the seventh anniversary of the killings found task force leader James Bell unusually optimistic. In an interview with the *Daily Herald* he was upbeat as he theorized that the passage of time might have actually become an ally. "Relationships change; friendships change," he said. "That can open up a whole new world in helping to solve it."

To bolster his theory, he offered a possible scenario: "There can be a bully in the neighborhood everyone is afraid of. He moves. Then people start telling you information." His notion could not be easily dismissed because of his many years of work as a case specialist at the FBI, during which, he noted, "We worked on cases 20 to 30 years old, and they got solved."

Though he didn't discuss it at the time, there was information less anecdotal on which to base his optimism.

What he and other law enforcement officials knew was that for the first time since the Brown's bodies were found, DNA testing technology had advanced to the point where it could now be used on the chicken dinner that crime scene analyst Jane Homeyer (who had since moved on to work for the FBI) had found in the garbage in the restaurant just hours after the bodies were discovered and so wisely kept frozen all these years. In late 1999, the chicken remains had been sent to the Illinois State Police crime lab for DNA analysis. Perhaps soon the test results would be in and help at last to identify a killer.

Though any viewer of television cop and lawyer programs is familiar with DNA, as in "We've got the DNA and it's a match," most don't know exactly what deoxyribonucleic acid actually is. Simply stated, it is a strand of genetic material packed in pairs in the nucleus of human cells that determines a number of inherited traits that control the body's chemistry and health. While scientists have known of the existence of DNA for more than a century, the first DNA profiling test was not developed until 1985, by Sir Alec Jeffreys, an Englishman. A year later he used DNA testing to identify Colin Pitchfork as the murderer of two young girls in the English Midlands. Perhaps just as important, the test was used during the course of that investigation to exonerate an innocent suspect.

Among the first uses of DNA test results in an American criminal trial occurred in Florida in 1987 when Tommy Lee Andrews was convicted and sentenced to ninety-nine years in prison for a series of sexual assaults. Now widely regarded as one of the most powerful crimefighting tools ever developed, DNA testing can be used to compare the unique genetic profile of the human body through analysis of blood, hair, saliva, skin, or semen.

The first DNA profiling test that was developed, though sophisticated and considered remarkably accurate, took several months to complete and required a large and relatively pure sample for the testing process. This testing process, called Restriction Fragment Length Polymorphism (RFLP), produced powerful results because it was so discriminating. For example, in the Andrews trial in Florida, prosecutors argued that the odds of the DNA belonging to someone else were 1 in 10 *billion*.

But while the RFLP test was an extremely powerful tool, it was of limited value because it required as many as fifteen thousand cells' worth of DNA. Further, the test could not be conducted on broken DNA strands or DNA strands damaged by exposure to the weather. The test was primarily limited to examining blood and semen that forensic analysts recovered in larger amounts—it could not be used to examine tiny specks of blood or the invisible saliva left on cigarette butts or on the back of a postage stamp.

Palatine police were familiar with the RFLP method, and unlike many law enforcement jurisdictions, the force had embraced it early as a legitimate and valuable tool. The force had first relied upon DNA testing in 1990 when a newborn baby was found floating, apparently drowned, in Salt Creek in Palatine.

It took only days to focus on a suspect—Elizabeth Ehlert, a woman who lived in a home next to the creek. Ehlert was still considered a suspect in the stabbing death of her mother two years earlier, but police had no evidence to link her to the murder. So, when the baby's body was found, Chief Bratcher had ordered that DNA tests be done on the blood extracted from the baby's body and on a sample of Ehlert's blood. Four months later, the tests provided the link necessary to charge Ehlert with murder. She was later convicted and sent to prison. At the time, prosecutors argued that Ehlert had never wanted the baby, had attempted to hide it by telling others she had a tumor, and then, after it was born, killed it by throwing it into the creek. Prosecutors later attempted to use DNA testing to try to prove Ehlert killed her mother, but they could not establish a connection and the murder was never solved. (In 2002, Ehlert's conviction was set aside because prosecutors had failed to prove the baby was born alive. In February 2003, the Illinois Supreme Court agreed to review the case.)

During those early years, DNA testing procedures were not always well received in courtrooms. Some judges considered it an unproven science and would not allow results into evidence. Prosecutors, defense lawyers, judges, and people in law enforcement realized that when a test showed that the genetic pattern of a suspect matched the genetic pattern of the evidence, it meant the suspect *might* have been the source of the evidence. There were two basic questions that had to be answered: What are the odds that someone else has the same genetic profile as the suspect? How small do these odds have to be when conviction or acquittal hangs in the balance?

The first question was gradually answered as law enforcement and private testing concerns took exacting measures to verify the RFLP process. The second question was answered by judges generally taking the view that deciding the adequate odds was a matter for a jury to consider along with all other evidence in a case. At the same time, the science was continuing to evolve as analysts attempted to devise ways to speed up the testing process and to accurately test smaller amounts of DNA.

When lab analyst Jane Homeyer had grabbed the remains of the chicken dinner from the Brown's garbage,
she knew that the state of DNA testing had not yet advanced far enough to be performed on any substance left
on the chicken. Although the DNA that remained on the
chicken bones, skin, and gristle would have to have come
from the saliva of the diner, the amount of saliva left
behind would be microscopic, if any were left at all. After
all, what if the killer had ordered that meal and had picked
away at it with his fingers instead of biting off chunks?

After years of frustration and disappointment, it was
likely that the new advances in DNA technology encour-
aged Bell to believe he might be able to take the investigation to a new place—a place less filled with guessing
and speculation, a place where the killer or killers had
long been hiding and, presumably, feeling safer with each
passing year.

By 1992, the justice system began to embrace another
DNA testing procedure. The test, designed to overcome
the need for a large sample of DNA, was called Poly-
merase Chain Reaction (PCR). While this test could use
a sample much smaller than the other testing method—
fifty to one hundred cells' worth of genetic material instead of the fifteen thousand required by RFLP—it had
serious limitations. PCR testing was not quite as discriminating as RFLP. Scientists using PCR could say, for example, that the odds of an identified profile belonging to
more than one person were 1 in 20,000—still good, but
nowhere near as powerful as the 1 in 10 billion odds that
RFLP testing produced and not reliable enough for a criminal case. By 1994, though, the FBI's crime laboratory
had begun employing PCR testing, as did some individual

state police crime laboratories, on samples that were not large enough or were too degraded to be submitted for RFLP testing. While perhaps not usable in court, these PCR test results helped isolate possible suspects against whom other evidence could be developed.

The Illinois State Police Crime Laboratory had begun using the RFLP test in the early 1990s, and by the middle of the decade had begun converting to the PCR test. And scientists continued to work on the testing process in an attempt to devise ways to raise its accuracy by increasing the number of identifying markers that could be compared between two samples. Simply stated, the higher the number of markers compared, the better the odds of identifying the right assailant.

By the time law enforcement laboratories had come to embrace the PCR testing method, European scientists were focusing on a class of genes called Short Tandem Repeat (STR) that had the potential to make PCR just as discriminating as RFLP without the sample-size limitation. Private industry in the United States developed the equipment that enabled scientists to do the analysis quickly. In this process, the number of comparison markers used produced satisfactorily high odds—the discrimination power of the test had increased and so had the odds of it being accurate. Indeed, the STR genes are so highly discriminating that they can differentiate between all human beings that have ever lived. The development of the PCR-STR testing process gave law enforcement the ability to successfully compare DNA from a suspect to cells taken from the steering wheel of an automobile or in a headband, or from saliva found on cigarette butts, the back of postage stamps, discarded chewing gum, or toothpicks. The Illinois State Police Crime Laboratory began

to employ this process in the late spring and early summer
of 1998.

With this new test came the ability to examine, for the
first time, the chicken meal, which had, since the murders,
been stored in a freezer at the Palatine Police Department.

WITHIN EVERY CRIME LABORATORY CERTAIN PRO-
cedures must be followed with painstaking accuracy to
ensure the reliability of the final results. These precau-
tions begin the moment evidence arrives, when it is cat-
aloged and assigned to an analyst. Each analyst is
required to document every step of the examination—
be it tests for the presence of gunpowder residue or a
search for fingerprints. And within each laboratory,
there is also a pecking order for which cases are handled when—some are processed more quickly than others. This order depends on the urgency of the case at
hand. For example, if a suspect is in custody but has
not been charged, police have only a limited time—
typically seventy-two hours—before they must either
file a charge or release him. If there is evidence that
might link that suspect to a particular crime, analysts
would likely be asked to handle the testing on an expedited basis—in effect, leapfrogging that particular
testing process ahead of other evidence already in the
testing pipeline.

In 1998, the typical order of testing at the Illinois
State Police Crime Laboratory called for expedited testing in cases in which a suspect would be released if
some evidence could not be found immediately. In
those circumstances, DNA testing could be done in as
little as three days. However, without a request for ex-

pedited handling, the DNA testing process could take as long as six to eight weeks.

If there were no expedited cases in the lab, the analysts would first work on cases in which test results were required by a specific court date. The next priority was cases with no suspect in custody, but there was a high-profile element—such as a series of rapes or murders in the same geographic area. The cases with the least priority were those in which there was no suspect and that had not occurred recently. The Brown's massacre—being five years old and with no suspect—fell into that category.

And so, later in 1998, analysts at the Illinois State Police Crime Laboratory began the initial testing on the residue of the chicken meal. Remarkably, a DNA profile was identified from the saliva found on the chicken bones. The profile was identified as coming from a male. It was a breakthrough, but just how big a breakthrough wouldn't be known until the profile could be linked to a human being. That, investigators knew, would be an arduous and painstaking process. It began with a request to Homeyer for her DNA. Even though the initial test had produced a profile that belonged to a male, an abundance of caution prompted a request that her DNA be tested.

It wasn't Homeyer.

That's when analysts began comparing the DNA of the seven victims of the massacre to the DNA obtained from the chicken. Months passed as the tests were gradually carried out on samples of blood that had been drawn during the autopsies of the victims that were performed shortly after the massacre. Again, analysts

found that the profile of the DNA found on the chicken
bones did not match any of the victims.

And so, investigators began to broaden their search,
reaching back to past suspects in the case. The list began with Paul Modrowski, who was in prison for the
beheading murder of Dean Fawcett. Robert Faraci,
Modrowski's codefendant, who had been acquitted of
the Fawcett murder, was stopped in the parking lot of
his apartment building. Police tracked down Martin
Blake, the former Brown's employee who had appeared
to be a strong suspect in the early hours of the case.
(Blake had sued for false arrest and settled for what he
later said was $8,000, after legal fees.) And they took
a sample from the man who had changed his story about
being in the restaurant on the night of the murders. In
each case, an investigator swabbed the inside of each
man's cheek, gathering cells containing their DNA to
compare to the DNA found on the chicken. This was
usually not difficult to do. Most of the men cooperated,
especially when told that if they did not, a court order
could compel them to do so. And, as one investigator
later noted, "How does it look if you are asked to give
up your DNA and you refuse? A guilty conscience,
maybe?"

That's when the task force's secret finally leaked out.
Chicago Tribune reporters Eric Ferkenhoff and Monica
Davey broke the story in April 2000—more than a year
after the initial testing of the evidence had begun—following interviews with Modrowski's lawyer and with
Faraci and Blake. The explanations the investigators
had given to the men whose DNA they were requesting
varied. One was told it was part of a routine review of
the case. Another was told that new technology was

allowing the investigators to take a fresh look at the evidence in the case.

Faraci said he agreed to give up his DNA, but only after he extracted a promise. "I told them that I would, but that they would have to publicly clear me," he said. The detective, he said, replied, "Oh, no problem."

The media were left to speculate about the specific evidence that had yielded the DNA the investigators were trying to match, since no one in the press and only a few in law enforcement even knew of the partially eaten chicken dinner that had been saved on the day the bodies were discovered.

Bell refused to comment on the *Tribune* reports. So did Cook County state's attorney Richard Devine. "We aren't commenting on suspects or commenting on evidence," said Palatine police chief Jack McGregor. "We are trying to maintain the integrity of the investigation. We've been consistent on that." Still, he exhibited a positive air. "I have always been optimistic this is a solvable case," he added. "The task force continues to investigate."

James Kearney, director of the Illinois State Police Crime Laboratory, confirmed for the press that tests were being conducted, but would not be specific about *what* was being tested.

The *Tribune,* citing unnamed sources, disclosed just days after its first report that the evidence had come from the residue of the meal—chicken, fries, a biscuit, and a drink—found in the garbage. Investigators had long believed it was a meal ordered by the killer because it matched the last receipt of the day that was time-stamped a few minutes after closing. They theorized that the killer had talked employees into sell-

ing the meal as a way of remaining inside until all other
customers were gone.

This led to the conclusion that the DNA profile was
the killer's. "Right now, we really like it," one unnamed
investigator told the *Tribune*. "We don't have any reason to believe it's not his. We can't account for it being
anyone else's."

But as summer approached, investigators found
themselves with nothing but a list of about a dozen
eliminated suspects. The DNA profile had been entered
into the Illinois DNA database—the repository of DNA
profiles taken from convicted felons as well as DNA
profiles from unsolved cases where a profile had been
identified but not yet matched to anyone—and the national database. No match was found.

"We have a profile," Kearney said, summing up the
state of the investigation as it settled into a new century.
"Who it belongs to, we have no idea."

TWENTY-SEVEN

I T WAS A SIMPLE INDICTMENT: "WITHOUT MERIT."
Using those words repeatedly, the expert panel assembled by the Illinois State Crime Commission issued a
report of its investigation of the BGA report. The forty-
eight-page document was issued in August 2000, nearly
three years after the BGA report had blistered the task
force and members of the police department.

"The Palatine Police Department and Brown's Chicken
Task Force and its members acted professionally, followed all leads and conducted the investigation thoroughly," the report concluded. "In short, the Better
Government Association's conclusions are not based upon
fact."

"There's no way this investigation was botched," said
Aldo Botti, an attorney who headed the team that conducted the review. "We looked behind the criticism and
we found that the BGA report—95 percent of it—was
baseless. We found the Palatine Police Department and

the other law enforcement agencies worked properly; they had harmony. A superb, investigative, follow-through job. We have no criticism. Unfortunately, some crimes never get solved."

The conclusions came as no surprise, as bits and pieces of the report had been leaking to the media for several days prior to its official release. Naturally, the BGA's executive director, Terrence Brunner, was ready to fire back, branding the review of his report an "irresponsible, reckless cheap shot" that was politically engineered by people biased in favor of the police. He pointed out that Mayor Rita Mullins was on the board of the ISCC. "We're not giving an inch on any of it," he declared. "They say we're wrong on stuff I know we have 15 ways from Sunday."

Mullins hailed the report as a vindication. "It speaks for itself," she said. "It certainly tells the rest of the world what I've always known—that the Palatine Police Department is very professional and have done everything they could in this investigation."

The report featured interviews with numerous officers from the task force. There was one notable exception, Chicago homicide detective Richard Zuley, who had so vigorously championed the controversial Lead 80. Zuley declined to participate. Perhaps he considered it a waste of time. As it turned out, the report concluded that further investigation of Lead 80 would have been a waste of time as well.

"Early on, Lead 80 was a viable lead which soon unraveled," the report said. Further, the task force had obtained the services of an independent police officer to come in to review it. "The officer, who requests anonymity, reached the conclusion that Lead 80 simply did not pan out and that the Palatine Police Department did not ignore this lead nor did individual egos in any way hinder the investigation."

The BGA's report was addressed point by point; its findings were repeatedly characterized as "without merit" and, at one point, described as "replete with innuendo and irrelevant material." The BGA report was even wrong on basic information, such as the rank or assignment of certain officers, the panel concluded.

The report said the BGA's description of the crime scene was incorrect. "There was no parade in the restaurant," it said. The only personnel allowed inside were employees of the medical examiner's office, the lead investigators, and crime scene technicians. All were required to wear protective clothing that included gloves and booties over their shoes. The report also dismissed the assertion that cooking oil had been slopped all over the premises. The fact, the ISCC report stated, was that a four-inch-wide pool of the oil had been spilled on the third or fourth day of investigation and it had had no detrimental impact on the crime scene's integrity.

All the victims had been fingerprinted, the canvassing of the area had not been bungled, and the crime lab had performed its duties in a professional and proper fashion, the report concluded. "Every possible witness was interviewed and some were re-interviewed," it said. "In reference to the media's report that persons who were in the area at the time of the murders were never interviewed, the [ISCC] determined that the persons making this claim were indeed interviewed and none of them provided information that could assist the investigators in solving the murders."

The fact that an officer tried the back door and thought it was locked when it was, in fact, not, which led to the failure to discover the bodies earlier, was "most unfortunate," the report said. The steel door was examined and determined to have a very tight frame and required "great pressure" to pull open. Without someone making such an effort, the door would indeed have appeared to be locked. Further, autopsies showed that the victims had died almost immediately, between 9:30 P.M. and 10:30 P.M. The failure to discover the victims when the police first visited a little after 1 A.M. would not have saved anyone's life.

Instead of finding, as the BGA had done, that Palatine police officers' egos and their inexperience had hamstrung the case, this report found a "dedicated, experienced, professionally-operated investigation." The report dismissed the BGA's charges that then chief Bratcher had used the case to further his outside consulting business and concluded that he had done nothing improper.

The report also dismissed the BGA's depiction of the task force as a group of "Argentine Army generals with chests full of medals" but no experience as "unfounded and an unfortunate erroneous characterization." While the ISCC panel had found "some differences of opinion expressed during the investigation, these varying opinions did not interfere with, jeopardize, delay nor impede this ongoing investigation."

The report noted that at the end of the first year of the investigation of the murders, the task force had brought in two experienced investigators to conduct a "cold-case review." Such reviews are frequently done on aging cases to ensure that nothing of significance has been overlooked. Typically they are conducted by individuals with no knowledge of the case so that all the information they review is fresh, no matter how old it really is.

Kirk Mellecker, a retired Los Angeles homicide detective whose cases included killers known as the Hillside Strangler, the Ski Row Stabber, the Freeway Strangler, and the Night Stalker, conducted a one-week review along with Ray Biondi, a retired Sacramento sheriff's homicide investigator, and Dr. Henry Lee, the Connecticut forensic scientist made famous in the O. J. Simpson case. The three had concurred, the report said, with the task force's theory of the case. Mellecker "determined that a complete and through job was done investigating suspects, performing investigative tasks, preserving evidence and utilizing 'ALL' tools available."

For instance, the report noted, the task force held three roll calls daily to ensure that information was shared among all officers. The FBI's Rapid Start Team was brought in during the first week of the investigation and computers were set up to capture information. In the first months after the murders, seventeen data loaders worked three shifts, twenty-four hours a day, to record the data and keep it current. And the FBI had provided its white-collar crime unit to review all of the restaurant's books and records to trace transactions that occurred on or about the date of the murders in an attempt to determine whether there was a financial motive behind the killings.

"Biondi was most impressed with the fact that the Palatine Police Department continues in its efforts to solve the crime while most other departments would tend to come up with reasons to put it aside," the report said. Further, Biondi said that Lead 80 "fell apart from the first page."

In its final analysis, the report concluded, "Illinois and other states have sentenced individuals to death for crimes they did not commit. They were later exonerated because of impermissible conduct by certain police personnel, prosecutors, or because of ineffective defense counsel. It is a tribute to the Palatine Police Department and the investigative agencies participating in the Brown's Chicken murder investigation that they did not, due to public outcry, rush to judgment and make arrests without proper proof. The Palatine Police Department, its chief, and all law enforcement agencies and members involved in the Task Force should be lauded, not criticized."

It was a hollow victory for Palatine and the task force, given that the killings remained unsolved. "Due to the horrific and appalling nature of this crime, we realize that we will always be open to speculation and conjecture on the part of others," said Chief Jack McGregor. "However, we remain focused."

TWENTY-EIGHT

THE SUN WAS THROWING LONG MORNING shadows as five men slowly approached the building that stood at 168 Northwest Highway in Palatine.

Some carried sledgehammers and crowbars. One sat atop a backhoe. When they reached a corner of the building, they stopped. Without exchanging glances or words, the men bowed their heads in prayer and except for the rush of traffic along the nearby streets, all was quiet on the early morning of April 27, 2001, when the Brown's building came down.

It had been shuttered for about eighteen months. The dry cleaners had operated in it for less than a year, clearing out in 1995. Plans for the delicatessen had halted in midrenovation. The possibility that a memorial would be constructed on the site had fizzled out. So even though the building only partially resembled the original restaurant—the facade had been remodeled—it had become an

eyesore, especially as other businesses around it flour-
ished.

"It should have come down a long time ago," said Laurie Mitchell, owner of the Edelweiss Delicatessen and Ca-
tering, which occupied space in the shopping plaza near
the building. "It is time to move on. Hopefully, this will
bring a sense of closure."

Even though the owner of the property on which the
restaurant stood claimed when putting the building up for
sale that it was one of the best retail spots in the village,
there had been no takers. But then Guido Tenuta, owner
of the Euro Fresh Plaza behind the former Brown's building, listened to the urging of his customers who told him
they thought the building should be torn down. So, for
$475,000, Tenuta bought the five-thousand-square-foot
property that included a portion of the Brown's parking
lot, intending to level the building and turn the entire plot
into a parking lot.

"My customers keep telling me they think we did the
right thing," said Tenuta. "Finally, I said, 'I don't want to
look at this building for the rest of our lives.' At least by
doing this we close the dark pages on those people's
lives."

Roy Marzano, owner of the realty company that listed
the property, said the building had been difficult to sell.
A few months earlier, he had told the *Daily Herald*, he
had to open the building to let inspectors inside, and they
had acted as if it were haunted. Tenuta himself had been
unsettled by its past. After the sale was completed, he had
refused to take the keys to the building.

"Frankly, this was the only buyer that made sense,"
said Bruce Blank, a realtor at the firm that sold the building. "People have tried to remodel, renovate and it just

never worked. It was impossible to counteract the stigma of what happened there. Prospective buyers, upon learning the history of the building, had always backed away. They would say, 'Well, I wouldn't want my wife working there. Or my daughter going there.' "

Many of those who continued to work in the immediate area had strong memories. In the days before the scheduled demolition of the building, Hermine Guerentz told the *Herald* that every day, when she looked out of the windows of the Edelweiss Deli where she worked, she was reminded of the dark, snowy day in 1993 when the bodies were taken out. "I see that back door every day," she said. "I can't get it out of my mind. I still think about it every day. And when it snows, it really reminds me. I'm glad it's being torn down."

Mayor Mullins hoped the demolition would provide some relief to the entire community. "It will finally erase the physical memory of the crime," she said. "It won't do anything to totally wipe it away, but it will go a long way. I wouldn't say it's closure. It softens the edges a little. Closure will come when the perpetrator is found and the who and why is determined."

The village was so eager to get rid of the building that it picked up the $25,000 tab for the demolition. Village manager Michael Cassady justified the expense, saying it was "appropriate in the vein of economic development. There was just too much baggage with that existing facility to further promote a strong, viable, commercial enterprise."

The families of the victims had mixed reactions to the demolition plan. Emmanuel Castro said he was pleased and relieved. "Part of me died in that building," he told

the *Chicago Tribune*. "For the family members, that
building is a painful building."

A regular customer of Tenuta's grocery, Castro said he
still drove by the building frequently but he wasn't dis-
appointed that a memorial had not materialized. "Why
live in the past?" he said. "It's better to move forward.
The memories are always there anyway. No one can erase
it, so just live with it. What's the choice? For me, there
is no choice."

Jennifer Shilling, whose parents, Richard and Lynn Ehlenfeldt, had owned the franchise, was wistful. While the
site was "obviously a scar for the community," she preferred planting trees or creating a park. By then married
and a Democratic state representative from the Wisconsin
city of La Crosse, Shilling said, "Something live would
be great."

Frank Portillo believed the building should have remained until a business finally took a chance. "Personally,
I think knocking the building down and getting it off the
tax rolls and employment rolls means that the bad guys
won," he said. Diane Clayton, whose son, Marcus Nellsen, was killed there, said, "The building itself had nothing to do with the murder. I can't say it's the building's
fault."

But the destruction was big news and television
crews—there were two news helicopters hovering over-
head—and reporters swarmed through the spectators on
hand to watch the early morning demolition. Palatine resident Dee Henriksen told *Herald* reporter Natasha Korecki
that she drove by the site every day. "It's sad. And I'm
just a person knowing we all at this time have something
in common. Why can't human beings, why can't we all
just get along?"

Mullins told the *Herald:* "Upon reflection, the Brown's incident was a defining moment in my life as well as the historical perspective of the community of Palatine. The small-town-security feel of my hometown was shattered and our innocence was lost. If this violent act could happen in middle America—the village of Palatine—it could happen anywhere. How true that proved to be. Palatine is now only one of many communities scarred by violence since that fateful winter day, Jan. 8, 1993."

For *Herald* photographer Mark Welsh, the demolition rekindled the memory of the day when he was assigned to cover the removal of the bodies from the restaurant. "I was out there from the very beginning and to the very end," he said. "It was just so God-awful cold out there that day. This morning [of the demolition], it was *deja vu* all over again to a certain extent. It just brought back that cold January day where it was bitterly cold. That day I was out there from 7 A.M. to like 11 P.M. We were all waiting and the rumors and the gossip were flying like everything. When they finally came out with the bodies, it was like a barrage of electronic flashes going off, they kept on bringing the bodies—not in a row, there was a delay between them, but they kept bringing them out. It was pretty overwhelming to see all that, all covered up, knowing there were bodies under there and five, or like eight hours earlier, they were alive." He added, "I'm glad it's being finally torn down."

As the demolition team finished its prayer, Ted Av-goustis, the general contractor, said, loud enough for the spectators to hear: "God bless their souls."

The backhoe fired up its engine and advanced on the portion of the building where the men had just prayed, the portion of the building where the seven bodies were discovered on that long-ago January morning. With a deliberate thrust, bricks began to crumble amid a cloud of dust. Some in the crowd carried still and video cameras to record what they must have felt was an historic moment in Palatine history. Some wept as they tried to talk about their memories of the murders. Others just stood silently.

Mary Jane Crow, whose brother, Michael Castro, had been among the seven victims, was at the site before the demolition began. At first she remained apart from the crowd, standing silently with her husband. Finally, realizing that reporters were waiting to hear her thoughts, Crow spoke, telling Korecki that she found herself in turmoil now that the day had arrived. "Today, I thought I'd be so happy about it, but once I saw it, it all came back," she said, tears streaming down her cheeks. "I was here the day it happened, and I remember waiting for them to bring out my brother. I can never forget that."

Hearing the demolition crew say a prayer before beginning their work "took my breath away," Crow would recall later. "I was so touched by it. And they began by tearing down the part of the building nearest where the bodies were found."

Later, she would not remember seeing any other family members of victims in the crowd, but she did remember that her husband, Steve, walked over to talk to one of the workmen and she remembers being "filled with rage." Without a word, she abruptly left the crowd and walked around the construction fencing and across the parking lot. She spoke to Avgoustis briefly. He nodded and ordered the backhoe's engine shut down, creating a palpable silence.

Avgoustis nodded toward Crow. She stepped toward the building and knelt to pick up a red brick from the rubble pile. She walked to the other side and stopped. There is no knowing exactly what she was thinking—what images might have been in her head. Did she stand there remembering the body bags being hauled out, wondering which one contained her lifeless brother?

There is no knowing which horrible memory was the one that provoked the piercing shriek that came from her mouth, or what force it was that compelled her to reach back and heave the brick from her hand through the air. It hit the glass window of the building squarely, shattering it into a hundred jagged pieces.

The crowd of onlookers gasped and then stared in amazement as Crow frantically scrabbled to pick up pieces of brick and rubble. Handful after handful, she hurled at the building, and as her arm rose and fell, she began to weep, sobbing so hard her body began to tremble. The bricks she threw shattered more windows and then she walked to a door and began pounding on it.

For a moment, no one moved. Then her husband approached his wife and grasped his arms around her in a firm hug. He held her tightly, her arms pinned to her sides. He lifted her off the ground, turned, and with her tears falling onto his jacket, carried her back around the fence and into the crowd.

The backhoe engine roared once more and the machine advanced on the building again. The men used their sledgehammers and their crowbars with a determined efficiency.

Crow and her husband left and went to work. They owned a Dairy Queen not far from the site. "I was off that day but I was so full of emotion that my husband said I should work. I didn't close up until later in the night and I remember my last customer complaining about life in the Midwest and I wanted to say, 'You have no idea what I went through today,' " she later recalled.

She drove by the demolition site on her way home and saw that the work crew was still at it. There were only a few people in the crowd watching. She would be home by the time the backhoe finally fell silent and the building in which her brother and six others had died had been reduced to a pile of rubble. The following day, Avgoustis sent trucks that began to load up the boards, plastic, bricks, and concrete, taking it all away once and for all.

TWENTY-NINE

WHEN THE TELEPHONE RANG, KATHLEEN PARker would remember with the same precise certainty one remembers the moment of a child's birth. It was 5:45 P.M. The date was March 25, 2002.

"Hello," she said, putting down the pen with which she was writing checks to pay an assortment of accumulated bills. She was twenty-six years old and living in a suburb north of Chicago. She fished a Marlboro Light out of its pack, flicked her lighter, and took a drag.

Parker immediately recognized the voice on the other end. It was that of her friend Anne Lockett, and she settled in for what she assumed would be one of those how's-everything-going-and-what's-new-with-you chats in which old friends often engage.

The two had known each other since both were freshman at Fremd High School in Palatine and found themselves making fun of a classmate who was passing notes. And when they were assigned to share a locker that year, it felt as if they were fated to be friends. It was a friendship that had lasted through their high school years and now, almost a decade later, continued as one of those on-again-off-again relationships that picks up without missing a beat, no matter the length of the interlude between conversations.

Little, even now, is known about Parker's life after high school, but it is well documented that on March 25, 2002, Lockett was living in Charleston, a city of twenty thousand about two hundred miles southwest of Chicago. The drive there on Interstate 57 passes corn and soybean fields, hog farms and rural towns. Charleston is a quiet place with the usual complement of bars, fast-food joints, and coffee shops that cater mostly to the faculty and ten thousand students at Eastern Illinois University.

Lockett was living in a modest apartment above a karate studio situated on the sleepy town square. She had been living in Charleston since 2000. She had left Palatine not long after graduation from high school to live for a time in Warrenton, Oregon, where her parents had previously moved and where her father had taken ill. After his death, Lockett had moved into a trailer park in Mattoon, just west of Charleston, to live with her sister, Cynthia. By March 2002, she had moved into the apartment in Charleston and was enrolled at the university, taking psychology classes and working with developmentally disabled adults. She was living with her boyfriend, a U.S. Army reservist who talked of joining the Peace Corps. Her life, it appeared to those who knew her, seemed to be on a good and solid track.

But Lockett was, in a very real sense, haunted by her past. Only she will ever truly know how or why old fears and memories began to manifest themselves in the way they ultimately did, but sometime in 2001, she had gotten a telephone call from her mother saying that Jim Degorski, an old high-school boyfriend, had called. He was looking for Lockett's telephone number, she said. Lockett was stunned. "Do not give my number to him," she had told her mother. "I just don't want to talk to him."

That is perhaps when these memories began to bedevil her in ways they never had before. She talked about them with her boyfriend and with one of his friends. But they had no solution. Neither did her sister or—when Lockett called back to explain her abrupt behavior—her mother.

She certainly felt increasingly desperate to find a way to banish, or at least cope with, ghosts nearly a decade old. Perhaps that is why, as awkward as it might have been, and as potentially dangerous, she finally decided to reach out to her old friend from high school.

The timing was good. Parker had called and left a message on Lockett's answering machine a few weeks earlier, and when she didn't receive a call back just assumed that Lockett was busy and would get back to her when she had time to talk. This was, Parker assumed, the reason for the March 25 call. But within a few minutes, Parker could tell that this was not merely a social call. Lockett's voice was serious, as if she was choosing each word with great care. She was asking her old friend for a favor.

Sure, Parker said, and then listened as Lockett asked her if she would forward an anonymous letter to the police. Though Parker pressed for more details—What sort of letter? About what? Why the police?—Lockett was not initially forthcoming. But haltingly, gradually, she offered bits of further information. The letter related to a crime. It could not be postmarked from Charleston.

Perhaps in frustration, Parker suggested that Lockett

just make another call, this time to police, and leave an anonymous tip about whatever it was she wanted to talk about. But Lockett said she didn't want her voice to be on any police department recording, adding ominously that she wanted to say what she had to say by letter because she was afraid that she might be flirting with serious trouble.

Parker told Lockett that she had some friends in the Palatine Police Department. She believed she could talk to them and, without divulging Lockett's name and dilemma, figure out if there was any trouble she could get into—if Lockett would just tell her *what* the problem was.

I'm just not sure, Lockett said. This further frustrated Parker and made her determined to get at whatever it was her friend had to say. She began to probe for details. Finally, after a few minutes, and after a long pause and a sigh, Lockett's tone went from cautious and halting to firm and forthright: *Do you remember how I've told you a dozen times that if anybody ever called looking for me to tell them you didn't know where I was?*

Indeed, Parker did remember those words. After each instance, she thought to herself that Lockett was probably trying to dodge pesky bill collectors. Lockett said her situation was far more dire. The people she was trying to hide from, she told her friend, were Jim Degorski and Juan Luna.

Parker remembered them both. They were high-school classmates and, like the two girls, part of the crowd that used to work and hang out at a Hoffman Estates joint called Jake's Pizza. She knew that for about two years, Degorski had been Lockett's boyfriend and that they had spent much of their time smoking marijuana and hanging out by the Fox River and nearby forest preserves or in

Degorski's room in the basement of his parents' home. Parker remembered him as being a "control freak" and that Degorski had not liked her and continually told Lockett to keep away from her. That was the main reason Lockett and Parker had drifted apart their senior year. That same year, Lockett was briefly hospitalized at Forest Hospital in Des Plaines for what she later referred to as "family counseling."

Parker's memory of Luna was less detailed: he was Degorski's friend, he also worked and hung out at Jake's, and he was in a job-training class with Degorski.

What about them? Parker asked.

The story, as Lockett detailed it to Parker and later to police, makes it easy to understand the demons that had been tormenting her, if not how she had been able to live with them so long.

This is her story.

On the night of January 9, 1993, Degorski had called Lockett at Forest Hospital. "Watch the news," he said. "I did something."

The lead story on the 10 P.M. television news was the discovery of seven bodies in a Brown's restaurant. Lockett called her mother and asked her to save any articles from the newspapers about the killings.

A few days later, after she was discharged from the hospital, Lockett went to Degorski's home, where she found him with Luna. Sitting in Degorski's basement bedroom, the two told her how they had killed all seven people. The conversation lasted a long time and Luna was quite animated during it. Degorski was cool and matter-of-fact.

Luna said he had wanted to kill someone and Degorski said he would help him. They decided on the Brown's restaurant because Luna had once worked there and knew the layout. Perhaps more important, he knew there was no alarm system. They dressed in old clothes and shoes and brought lots of bullets. "Pockets full," Lockett told Parker. They took Degorski's snub-nosed .38-caliber revolver. They drove Luna's car and parked in a lot behind some town houses near the restaurant. They walked in a strange exaggerated gait through the snow to the restaurant, where they put a wedge in the back door so no one could run out. They went in just at closing and Luna ordered a chicken dinner. Degorski became upset because the chicken was greasy and he thought Luna might leave fingerprints. After Luna ate some of the chicken, both men put on gloves and pulled out a gun.

There was scuffle with one of the workers. Another worker tried to run out the back door, but it wouldn't budge. The worker then ran up front and jumped over the counter and was shot. That's when Luna and Degorski began to herd everyone into the coolers. Luna said that he shot one victim, but when the victim did not immediately die, Degorski finished him off.

Luna grabbed Lynn Ehlenfeldt around her neck, called her a bitch for doing something to the safe, and then cut her throat. As they were shooting people in the coolers, one of the victims had vomited french fries. With everyone dead, Luna and Degorski had cleaned and mopped up and left. They took the money. They later threw their clothes and shoes in separate garbage bins and tossed the gun in the Fox River at a place where Degorski had once taken Lockett fishing.

Several days later, Lockett was at Degorski's house when Luna telephoned. The Brown's task force wanted to talk to him, he said, because he had once worked at the restaurant. Degorski told Lockett to accompany Luna to the interview and that both should dress neatly to avoid suspicion. When the day of the interview came, Luna drove her to the station and they sat in a waiting room until a detective summoned Luna. He was back out in less than thirty minutes. No one asked Lockett any questions. As they were leaving, Luna told her that it had been easy and that they had photographed him.

Degorski and Luna had never talked about the murders again. The last time it was mentioned was when Degorski said this to Lockett: "If you ever tell anyone about this, I will kill you."

THIRTY

PARKER STUBBED OUT HER CIGARETTE AFTER hanging up the telephone. Lockett's story was astonishing, terrifying. She felt almost breathless. She looked at the clock and was surprised. What had seemed like only minutes had been a conversation of nearly an hour. The ashtray was almost full. Taking a deep breath, she picked up the telephone again and dialed the Palatine police station.

At the end of the conversation with Lockett, Parker had persuaded her to allow her to contact a police officer whom she had known for several years. After graduating high school, Parker had worked at a gas station for about six years, and during that time, she had come to be friendly with a half-dozen Palatine officers. "People would drive off without paying for their gas," she later recalled. "Sometimes they would just forget or sometimes they were trying to get away without paying. I would write down their plate numbers and call the police. There

were some of the same officers who would come out—
sometimes it happened once a week. I got to know them.
There was one in particular that I trusted."

When the dispatcher at the police station picked up
Parker's call that night, she asked for that officer. He was
not on duty, the dispatcher said. Parker asked for other
officers whom she knew. None were on duty. Parker then
asked the dispatcher to call the first officer at home and
ask him to call her. The dispatcher did. The officer returned the call.

"He was excited to hear it all," Parker later said. "I
asked him what liabilities would Anne have. He said
none." The officer said he would contact Palatine detective sergeant Bill King and have him call her back.

Parker hung up and waited nearly an hour before the
telephone rang again. It was Lockett. She wanted to know
what was going on. "The detective didn't call you back
yet?" she asked.

"No," Parker said. "But when he does, it is okay for
him to talk to you?"

They agreed that Lockett would talk to the detective,
but that Lockett wouldn't give him any personal information about herself. Then, after further discussion, Lockett agreed to let Parker give the detective the name Anne
and a phone number.

Parker called the station again and asked to speak to
the detective on duty. They spoke for just a few minutes
and then he said he would call Lockett. Parker was up the
entire night, waiting for some word, but she heard nothing.

The following day, March 26, Lockett called Parker
and said a detective named King had, indeed, called her
at home and reviewed her story with her. Detective King

had ended the conversation by promising that someone from the task force would get back to her.

Lockett's story seemed almost too good to be true. Particularly for King, who was one of the two remaining members of the task force and the only person who had been on the case from the day the massacre was discovered. He had listened carefully to Lockett's story and had come away convinced that she was probably telling the truth. But after so many false leads and suspects that turned out to be duds, he steeled himself against the possibility that he was embarking on just another wild-goose chase. But just as he had so many hundreds and hundreds of times before, he was determined to take this lead as far as it could go. This one was different, though, because Lockett knew something that had never been released or even leaked to the media—that one of the victims had vomited french fries during the shooting. That was something that only the real killers could have witnessed.

For Parker, the next two weeks passed at an agonizingly, fretfully slow pace. She wondered if the detective had even taken Lockett's story seriously. "They have had about 15,000 tips about this thing, but nothing had ever come of it," she later recalled. "He had received hundreds of phone calls about it, and I'm sure he thought this was just another tip that would lead to nothing."

Over these two weeks, Parker also became fearful. She realized she could well be a witness if Lockett's story resulted in a criminal prosecution. She and her roommate began locking doors and windows and double-checking to make sure they were locked.

Then John Koziol, who had been Palatine's chief of police since McGregor's retirement, showed up at Parker's apartment along with Cook County Sheriff's Police commander John Robertson and Scott Cassidy, an assistant Cook County state's attorney who headed the state's attorney's office cold-case unit. They questioned her for hours, searching for new details or for inconsistencies and holes in her story. "These guys were so on the ball. They went over every single nitty, gritty thing," Parker would recall. "They wanted to get in their car and drive to see Anne right then."

Parker looked at her watch and reminded them that it was 9 P.M. and that the drive to Charleston would take at least three hours. "Not a problem," one of them said. "Then they asked me to call Anne. But she wasn't answering the phone," Parker recalled. "So they didn't go."

During these weeks, Palatine police were hard at work. They pulled the investigative report of Luna's interview with the task force so many years before. One of about three hundred Brown's employees questioned in the days after the murders, Luna had said during his interview that on the night of the massacre he had been with a friend from high school. Her name, he had said, was Eileen Bakalla. The investigators had talked to Bakalla back in 1993 and she had confirmed that Luna was with her that night.

Like Lockett, Bakalla had been part of the Jake's Pizza crowd, although she was older than Degorski, Luna, and Lockett. But like Degorski, she had worked there making pizzas and waiting on tables. Diagnosed with Attention Deficit Disorder in the fourth grade, Bakalla had lived until her early teens in Buffalo Grove, a northwest suburb not far from Palatine. The family had then moved to Hoffman Estates, where she lived with her mother and stepfather. She, too, had attended Fremd High School.

Police tracked down the twenty-nine-year-old Bakalla and questioned her about her whereabouts on the night of the murders. Was she with Luna, as he and she had said?

In a fashion, yes, she said, she was with Luna. But not the way in which she had originally described during the task force interview nearly a decade before. Her story was as chilling as Lockett's.

She said she was working at Jake's when Degorski called on the night of January 8, 1993. He told her to meet him at a grocery store parking lot nearby. "We did something big," she recalled him saying. When she arrived, Degorski and Luna were in Luna's car. There were latex gloves on the console and Luna had a canvas bag. As they drove to her town house in Elgin, about eighteen miles south and west of Palatine, Degorski and Luna told her they had robbed the Brown's restaurant on Northwest Highway.

At the town house, Luna and Degorski split up the money that was in the bag and gave fifty dollars to Bakalla. The three smoked some marijuana, and in the pre-dawn hours of January 9, she drove them back to Luna's car at the grocery store lot, where she dropped Luna off. At Degorski's request, they drove by the Brown's restaurant, where they saw the flashing lights of police cars and ambulances.

The following day, she and Degorski picked up Luna's car and took it to a car wash, where Degorski cleaned it, inside and out. A few days later, she and Degorski went shopping together with the money from Brown's. He had a roll containing several hundred dollars and she had the fifty dollars they had given her. He bought clothes. She bought a pair of shoes.

With these two very similar stories from Lockett and Bakalla—stories that contained information that was known only to police and to the killer—police began looking for Luna and Degorski.

They found Luna in Carpentersville, a suburb northwest of Chicago. At first glance, he seemed to be an average citizen. Except for a bounced $100 check at a muffler shop in 1999 that had led to about $400 in fines, Luna's path never crossed that of the police. In 1994, while on a visit back to Mexico, he had met and fallen in love with a woman named Imelda. They married, came back to the United States, and moved into a one-bedroom apartment in the suburb.

Degorski, on the other hand, had always seemed to find trouble. In 1990, he was charged with burglary for breaking into a locker at a construction site; he was placed on court supervision and fined. In 1991, he was charged with possession of a stolen car, a charge later reduced to criminal trespassing. In 1992, he was charged with battery and unlawful restraint for repeatedly punching an eighteen-year-old ex-girlfriend and hauling her off in his car, where he allegedly held her prisoner for several hours until letting her go. Over the next eight years, Degorski had gone through a number of jobs, none of them paying particularly well. These included installing window shutters, working as an assistant janitor at a golf course, and operating his own business, Jim Of All Trades, which repaired and remodeled homes and boats and cleaned offices. He moved around to different Chicago suburbs, then to Arizona, then back to the Chicago area. Along the way, he had been convicted of marijuana possession and racked up several traffic violations, including driving under the influence of alcohol. Finally, in December 2000, he had moved to Indianapolis and found a construction job, telling a neighbor he was "tired of all the violence."

Palatine police approached Degorski and Luna separately and asked them to allow the inside of their cheeks to be swabbed for a DNA sample. Both men gave their permission with surprising ease. Luna was swabbed at his home. Degorski, amazingly, drove up to Palatine from Indianapolis so a lab technician could take the swab and swipe it against the inside of his cheek. If they were scared or suspicious of the reasons that the police needed their DNA, neither man displayed this to the officers. As one investigator later said: "It was easy for Luna—he had worked at Brown's and it didn't seem unusual that this was being done. For Degorski, I don't know. Maybe he thought that if he refused, he would look guilty. And if he had, we would have gotten a court order."

On May 8, the results of the DNA tests came back, hitting the task force like a bolt of lightning: the DNA profile from the chicken was a match to Luna. The odds of it being wrong were, the lab analysts said, 1 in more than a *trillion*.

Investigators went back to Lockett on May 11. You need to help us, they said. You need to call Degorski. Tell him you are being asked about the murders. Ask him what you should say to police.

She came to Chicago, where she testified before a Cook County grand jury. With her story locked in under oath, the investigators obtained a court order to allow them to listen in on a telephone call she would make to Degorski. Using as a ruse Degorski's previous attempt to find Lockett by calling her mother in Oregon, Lockett called him back. A tape player recorded every word of their conversation. Parker would later recall that Lockett told her that Degorski "wasn't shocked to hear from her. He didn't say anything like, 'Wow, Anne, how did you get my number?' He actually apologized to her, saying 'I'm sorry I got you involved. I'm sorry that the police are hounding you.' "

Never once did Degorski admit to being involved in the Brown's massacre. But neither did he deny it. All of which led police to believe he had been involved. Though neither he nor Luna had the sort of life or background— the "profile," as the experts might call it—that would suggest either one was a mass murderer, that is what the police believed they were. And on May 16, 2002, fifty-two days after Lockett's chilling call to Parker, Palatine police arrested James Degorski and Juan Luna.

THIRTY-ONE

O N THAT THURSDAY AFTERNOON, LUNA HAD gotten off from his job as an installer of dishwashers and refrigerators at Gulgren TV and Appliance in the suburb of Crystal Lake and driven to Carpentersville, where he picked up his four-year-old son from kindergarten. He stopped to buy gas at a station near his family's apartment. His wife, Imelda, was waiting for him to pick her up so she could drive him to a job interview. Even though he already worked six days a week, Luna was hoping to get a second job so the family could save enough money to buy their own home.

Meanwhile, in Indianapolis, Degorski was ending his workday for Associated Services Inc., where he spent most of his time repairing the exteriors of storm-damaged condominiums. He had moved from Arizona earlier in the year and was living in a brick ranch home with his brother. Degorski was in the company parking lot, unloading tools from his work truck into his personal truck.

Neither man would make it home that night.

Both men had been under twenty-four-hour surveillance since May 8, when the DNA profile from the chicken was determined to be Luna's. When the word had come from the Illinois State Police Crime Laboratory, Detective Bill King had summoned other Palatine officers and they had walked into the office of Chief John Koziol, where King announced the lab finding. There had been no joyous whoops or hand-slapping that day. Jaded by the years and years of dead-end leads and bogus suspects, they knew that there was always a possibility that something could go wrong. And so they had set about devising a plan.

That plan had included the secret taping of the conversation between Lockett and Degorski—a call that had not given them what they really wanted—a full-blown admission of his participation in the massacre. At the same time, they scrambled to assemble surveillance teams. Two men were assigned to watch Luna and two men were dispatched to Indianapolis to keep an eye on Degorski. They were ordered to rent a truck or a car and to change vehicles every day so that Luna and Degorski would not become familiar with the vehicles and perhaps figure out they were being watched and decide to flee. Now the moment came to swoop down. Four more officers were dispatched to Indianapolis to assist in the arrest of Degorski. Others were sent to back up the team assigned to Luna.

As Luna stepped out of his car at the gas station, officers with guns drawn approached him, told him he was under arrest, and placed him in handcuffs. Another officer took his son so he could be driven home to his mother.

More than two hundred miles away, as Degorski stood next to his work truck, two unmarked cars pulled up and several men stepped out. They approached Degorski, frisked him, and led him to one of the cars. The detectives gave him the choice of accompanying them willingly— which meant no handcuffs—and he obliged. Degorski, a coworker would later recall, looked at him, shrugged his shoulders, and ducked into the backseat of the car for the long ride back to Palatine.

Both men were questioned separately. Their interrogation would continue on into Friday morning. Not surprisingly, given the growing optimism within the Palatine Police Department, word began to leak out to the press toward the end of the day on Thursday that suspects in the Brown's massacre case were being questioned.

On Thursday night, the *Chicago Tribune* found Cook County state's attorney Dick Devine at home. Devine confirmed that two suspects were being questioned but would not discuss specifics. He said no charges had been filed. At this point, the situation was identical to what had transpired over and over in the past nine years since the massacre. And there was no reason to think that these arrests would end up any differently than their predecessors. No reason, that is, until Devine offered an assessment of the ongoing interrogation.

"This isn't pie in the sky," he said. "This is not a flier. This is serious."

On Friday morning the front-page headline in the *Tribune* made a statement that many Chicago area residents and not just a few law enforcement authorities had once believed would never be made: 2 HELD IN 1993 BROWN'S KILLINGS.

That Friday proved a long day for family members of the victims. Diane Mennes, sister-in-law at Thomas Mennes, said: "The cops didn't tell us very much." She and her husband, Jerry, said it was too early to get their hopes up. "They've had a couple of suspects before, and it didn't pan out," she said. "So that's why we're waiting. But if it's legit, then we're going to be really happy."

For years, Joy McClain had regularly stopped by the Palatine Police Department just to see if there had been any developments in the murder of her fiancé, Marcus Nellsen. Coincidentally, she had dropped in that morning, but officers informed her that the detectives were unavailable and wouldn't be able to get back to her for several days.

"And then this happens," McClain told the *Tribune*. "I'm just keeping my fingers crossed that it all doesn't blow up and it's all a mistake. All I want to know is why—what went on and what happened?"

On Saturday morning, Degorski and Luna were driven from the Palatine Police Department to the Cook County Criminal Courts building, where they appeared for a bond hearing.

Prosecutor Linas Kelecius, a member of the state's attorney's cold-case unit, delivered a summary of the state's evidence before the court and a hushed crowd of reporters. His delivery was dry and methodical. "Your honor," he began, addressing Cook County Circuit Court judge Mary Margaret Brosnahan. "We would like to start out by pointing out that this is a capital case in that the defendants murdered seven people and did so during the course of an armed robbery.

"They committed these murders on January eighth, 1993, shortly after nine P.M. at the Brown's Chicken restaurant at 168 West Northwest Highway, Palatine, Illinois."

Then he read a list of the dead: "The people killed are

Michael Castro, age sixteen; Guadalupe Maldonado, age
forty-eight; Marcus Nellsen, age thirty-one; Rico Solis,
age seventeen; Lynn Ehlenfeldt, age forty-nine; Richard
Ehlenfeldt, age fifty-two; Thomas Mennes, thirty-two."

Kelecius told the judge that Degorski and Luna had
been "talking about pulling something like this for quite
some time. That particular Friday, they decided to actually
do it."

When the robbery began, chaos erupted, Kelecius said.
"People started running. One man ran for the back door
and couldn't get out because the doorjamb was in there.
They started shooting everybody."

Luna, Kelecius said, had shot Lynn Ehlenfeldt, Michael Castro, Rico Solis, Guadalupe Maldonado, and Marcus Nellsen in one cooler. When one victim—which one
was not clear, but it was either Castro, Solis, Maldonado,
or Nellsen—did not immediately die, Degorski took the
gun and pumped yet another shot into him. Then Degorski
walked to the other cooler and shot Richard Ehlenfeldt
and Thomas Mennes. A total of twenty-one shots were
fired, Kelecius said, forcing the two to reload the weapon
at least three times. Degorski and Luna collected all the
expended shells and left. As they crossed the parking lot,
they retraced their steps, carefully walking in the footprints in the snow that they had left on the way into the
restaurant.

"There is absolutely no doubt that they committed
these murders," Kelecius said. He said that both men had
made admissions. Luna had done so on videotape, while
Degorski had given an oral admission and started to give
a videotaped statement, but then abruptly halted the taping
almost as soon as it began. Perhaps he realized the powerful impact a taped statement would have in a courtroom

before a jury. It didn't really matter at that point—he wasn't going anywhere.

Kelecius read from the confessions, revealing for the first time the existence of Anne Lockett and Eileen Bakalla, but did not identify them by name, referring to Lockett as "Witness A" and Bakalla as "Witness B." He told of their accounts of how Luna and Degorski had bragged of the massacre and told the women how they committed it.

Speaking about Lockett, Kelecius said, "She is the hero who caused this case to be solved, and right-thinking people will recognize, one, she is a hero; two, that Degorski is the primary reason why she did not come forward until now. Degorski told her he would kill her if she ever told anyone. She believed this mass murderer would carry that threat out. It took courage for her to come forward. Also heroes are her friends and family who helped her make that decision."

At the conclusion of the hearing, Judge Brosnahan ordered both men held without bond.

That Friday afternoon, Palatine police chief John Koziol, accompanied by a phalanx of other law enforcement authorities, including former Palatine police chiefs Jerry Bratcher and Jack McGregor, stood in a room at the police department to publicly announce the filing of murder charges. Bratcher and Mayor Rita Mullins stood directly behind Koziol. The room was jammed with media and family members of the victims. The news conference was broadcast live on many of the area's television channels.

The moment was heavy with drama as Koziol spoke the words so many of those assembled had been waiting so long to hear. "Today the Palatine Police Department, along with the Cook County Sheriff's Police, the Cook

County State's Attorney's Office, and the Illinois State Police Crime Lab announce the arrest of James Eric Degorski and Juan A. Luna for the murder of seven workers at the Brown's Chicken and Pasta Restaurant on January eighth, 1993."

The room erupted in applause.

"Together," Koziol continued, "we have amassed a formidable case against these cold-blooded killers. This evidence includes sworn testimony, court-ordered overhears, admissions by the defendants, and, most importantly, DNA evidence. I want to acknowledge all the fine investigators and agencies who have assisted us over the many years in this case. There were over one hundred and fifty."

Koziol took a breath and looked directly into the television cameras.

"And to the people charged," he declared, his voice choked with emotion. "You wanted to do something big. I hope you are placed in a cage that you have built through your own inhumanity toward the innocent. I am confident that you will receive the death sentence you so justly deserve. It galls me that these two individuals, who are void of human conscience, took the lives of seven decent, law-abiding Americans. May those seven people, whose faces will forever be etched in our memory, now rest in peace."

One by one, other lawmen stepped forward and stood in front of the cluster of microphones.

Cook County Sheriff Michael Sheahan said, "This is a very difficult case. It's been a long time coming. Our department has been proud to be part of this investigation. From day one, the case has had a chilling effect on all of us in law enforcement, on all the people in this community and all the people in Cook County.

"The police never gave up," Sheahan continued. "They never forgot the victims and that's the key here. That's why it's such a great day to see these officers here and all the assistant state's attorneys, the sheriffs, and all the other officers who worked on the case tirelessly for a number of years—over nine years."

He took a verbal swipe at the Better Government Association's now discredited report, saying, "When you think of this case, there were, I believe—with the other chiefs and for Chief John Koziol—over the years, some unfair criticism. That unfair criticism was about a very difficult case. There were no eyewitnesses. All the victims were dead.

"Some people said some things they shouldn't have said," Sheahan said. "But we got a break, and with the young officers here and all the officers that worked on this case, it came at a great time. They all got together and they did great work, great police work, over the last several weeks. It's really a great day for all of us in law enforcement, and the people do win in the end."

Cook County state's attorney Richard Devine spoke next. "As Chief Koziol and Sheriff Sheahan said, today we announce charges against two individuals for seven murders. We kind of say that quickly, but when you stop and think of the terrible devastation that was brought to bear on many, many families—on a neighborhood, on a community—by that senseless and unforgivable act several years ago, we are all—I think it's fair to say we are gratified in one sense for the relatives of the victims, to the families, to whom our hearts go out.

"There's some relief, no doubt," Devine continued. "But there is no bringing back the loss of loved ones. To law enforcement, there is some satisfaction, but even more, there is a firm resolve that this case will be brought to a just and fitting conclusion. I want to say, particularly, thank you to the Palatine Police Department. They've lived with this every day for many years. It has been something they have seen as a burden in some senses, but they have never given up, and today shows the results of their tremendous and ongoing efforts.

"We remember the victims. We remember their families. And we do make the commitment to all of you that this case will be pursed and we will get justice in the end."

Devine said it was too soon to decide whether to seek the death penalty. "We have a process in our office that we follow. We will follow that process in this case, but I can say this was a horrible brutal series of murders and one that we look at in the most serious way possible." He added, "While there was a robbery involved, the basic motivation was to go in and to kill other human beings."

Asked to explain how Lockett came to talk to police, Kelecius stepped forward. "The police did not contact her," he said. "She reached out to police."

Koziol then interjected, "She spoke with a friend of hers who had a stronger moral compass than she did." That friend, Koziol said, referring to Kathleen Parker, "reached out to us. And she convinced her source to speak with us, so going to her friend gave her the strength to speak with us." He characterized Bakalla's reason for not coming forward as "a very tight friendship" with Luna.

Asked if either woman would be prosecuted, Devine replied, "These are witnesses. They are going to be witnesses in the case and I'm not going to comment beyond that." Koziol added, "We need all the witnesses in this case that we can get . . . They're on board in our case now and we intend to use them."

James Kearney, director of the Illinois State Police Crime Laboratory, explained how Luna's DNA had been found on the chicken bones. When he was asked about Jane Homeyer's decision to save the chicken, his understated response prompted applause: "Well, it's pretty good police work."

At the request of reporters, Koziol introduced Detective Sergeant Bill King. A nineteen-year police veteran, the forty-six-year-old King moved slowly to the lectern, his eyes blinking behind thick eyeglasses in the television lights, and gripped it with two weathered hands. King did not have the appearance of a detective who had doggedly worked on the case for nearly a decade, but of some friendly uncle who would have preferred to be reading a bedtime story to a niece instead of standing before the glaring TV camera lights.

"Can you tell us what you're feeling today?" a TV reporter asked.

"I'm feeling very happy for the families," King said, his voice soft. "I was pretty convinced when I heard some of the statements the lady made that we were looking at the right guys."

"What toll has this taken on you personally?" another reporter asked.

"I don't know that yet," said King, known to fellow officers in the Palatine Police Department as a man who didn't complain and regularly worked long hours. Then he thought for a moment and added, "It's my job and it's what I did."

Pressing for a more lively sound bite, another reporter tried it a different way. "With this lead, when was it that it snapped, like, 'Oh my God, we're actually going to do this?' And what was that like?"

"Well," King said, in his typically understated manner. "I think the DNA was really helpful. And like I said, everything just fell into place. I was hoping that some- thing would happen. It didn't matter if it was someone coming forward or some new evidence dropping in. If someone comes forward, it all snaps."

"In March," a reporter asked, "when they came for- ward, was it pretty clear to you: 'Wow, this looks like the real thing. It looks like we got them?' "

"Like I said before, it was very good information," King said, pointing to Lockett's knowledge that one of the victims had vomited french fries. "It was something we never released. And that was something the person told me and that became very interesting to me right away. And I went from there."

"And then, what was the thing that really convinced you?" the reporter persisted. "The DNA, the overhear? Was there one crucial piece of evidence?"

"Well," King said. "The DNA was very good, but I think the confessions are very good. And they match."

King stood at the podium for another moment, await- ing another question. One came, but it was intended for Koziol, who was asked to describe the demeanors of Luna and Degorski after they were brought in and during their interrogation. Koziol stepped forward. "Pretty noncha- lant," he said. "Your typical sociopath type. They never showed any remorse throughout their statements. I cannot explain their motivation for doing this killing. We still cannot give that answer to the families. They never really gave us one. They just did it to do something big. There's no explanation as to why they stopped. They are people without a soul."

THIRTY-TWO

THE RELATIVES OF THE DEAD REACTED WITH A mixture of relief and thanksgiving, as well as shock, anger, and bewilderment.

And they wanted justice in the extreme.

They were relieved and grateful that, at last, the men they believed were the killers of their loved ones had been caught. "We're finally able to exhale," said Jennifer Shilling, one of Richard and Lynn Ehlenfeldt's three daughters. "For the last nine years, it has felt like we were holding our breath."

"I have been fantasizing about this day for a long time," said Mary Jane Crow, sister of Michael Castro. "All I want to do is thank everybody."

Shilling added, "My family and I appreciate the hard work of the Palatine Police Department as well as the other law enforcement agencies that have always remained committed to solving this case."

All were bewildered as the details of the crime shed

new light on the final minutes of the victims' lives. "I've always had pictures in my head of what could have happened," said Crow. "Was my brother the first one? Was he the last one? Did he suffer? When you hear the actual details, it's not easy to swallow. I'm actually kind of happy and sad at the same time."

They were angry that relatives had died to fulfill the desires of two men to kill. "What a waste," said Joy McClain, who had been engaged to Marcus Nellsen. "Just to get a thrill, they butchered seven people. Those people must have been terrified when they realized what was going to happen."

They were bewildered that Luna and Degorski and Lockett and Bakalla had gone on after the massacre to live seemingly normal lives. Luna and Degorski apparently had remained relatively trouble-free while Lockett and Bakalla had not told authorities what they had known for so long.

"It's repulsive to me, and it's unconscionable to me to not have done that nine years ago," said Joyce Sojoodi, another of Richard and Lynn Ehlenfeldt's daughters, referring to Lockett and Bakalla.

"They're just saving their own butts, that's all," Crow told reporters. "It makes me sick to know a lot of people knew about it and just kept their mouths shut." She added, "These people came from Palatine. These people came from Fremd. I'm completely baffled. To think these people are that evil, I'm baffled."

Diane Mennes, sister-in-law of Thomas Mennes, voiced a different perspective, noting that had Lockett come forward prior to 1998—when DNA testing was not sophisticated enough to isolate a profile from saliva—their words might not have been enough to make a credible case against Luna and Degorski. "God works in mysterious ways," Mennes said. "If she would have come forward first, they probably would have thought she was loony tunes. A lot of people were coming forward at the time accusing their ex's."

Richard Ehlenfeldt's sister, Ann, concurred. "In my mind, I'm glad it happened now because I think there's more likely to be a conviction with the DNA evidence."

They wanted justice served. And for most, that meant the death penalty.

"They killed my son," said Emmanuel Castro. "That's what they deserve. If they're going to the electric chair, I'll put in the plug. I'll pull the switch. If they're given an injection, I'll give the injection. If they're given a firing squad, I'll pull the trigger." He told the *Daily Herald* that if he died and were given a choice, he would choose to go to hell rather than heaven—so he could torment Luna and Degorski for all eternity.

Dianne Mennes said she hoped Luna and Degorski would be executed in the same fashion as they were accused of killing in the restaurant. "For me, there is no penalty for what they did. Whatever they get is not good enough," said Marcus Nellsen's mother, Diane Clayton. "One of the suspects has a little boy. He's going to see what it's like to lose his son. But his son is still alive. I wish mine was."

While Chief John Koziol had declined reporters' invitations to discuss the now-infamous Better Government Association Report that had been so critical of the investigation, others were not.

"I'm sitting here today, saying, 'Where's the Puerto Rican gang members?' " said Jerry Elsner, director of the Illinois State Crime Commission, the group that had issued a report that praised the Brown's investigation and had labeled the BGA report as without merit. "I'm waiting for the apologies to come."

The BGA's Brunner stubbornly refused to give one, though. He said he stood by the group's report.

As he had done for so many years, former Palatine chief Jerry Bratcher thought of others before himself. "I don't need their apology," he said. "I've got enough scar tissue that I'm insulated. Maybe they should apologize to the law enforcement community and the people they misled."

Frank Portillo, the man whose dissatisfaction and frustration with the investigation had prompted the BGA report, seemed to be one of the few willing to acknowledge the obvious. "I know Chief Bratcher wanted to solve the crime just like anyone else. I feel bad I was a critic, and if I could do it all again, I'd take it back."

While the arrests brought some measure of closure and the apparent answers to questions that had long shadowed the case, there were now even more questions to which there seemed to be no answers.

What really could drive two young men with relatively nonviolent upbringings to commit mass murder?

How could they live such seemingly normal lives afterward?

How could those two young women keep their secret for so long?

The questions were asked over and over again, by the media, by relatives of the victims, on radio talk shows, in letters to the editor, and in conversations on the street. Heated debate ensued over whether Lockett or Bakalla was entitled to any of what had risen to $135,000 in reward money. Prosecutors had called Lockett a hero. Others, including family members of the victims, were angry and puzzled over her failure to come forward.

"It's a mystery to me and I'm sure to many other people," said Mayor Rita Mullins.

"How their conscience would let them go without talking to the police, how they could live with themselves, I have no idea," said Portillo. "What these people did was an act of cruelty." Asked about the reward fund, which included $50,000 he had pledged, Portillo said, "I'd burn it before I'd give it to anyone who waited nine years."

"I don't think people who waited should get any of it," Mary Jane Crow added. Joyce Sojoodi said, "I'm frustrated they didn't come forward before. They put us through a lot of anguish that didn't need to go on so long."

Some wondered aloud why Lockett and Bakalla were not being prosecuted themselves for obstruction of justice, even though the statute of limitations clearly barred the filing of such charges.

"What are we trying to accomplish here?" attorney William Belmonte, a member of the Illinois State Crime Commission's panel that investigated the BGA report told reporters. "Are we trying to punish a class four felony or are we trying to get two guys for a potential capital punishment murder of seven people? I don't think the people should be too worried about punishing the girls as they should be about punishing the two guys."

The public pressure prompted lawyers for Lockett as well as Bakalla and her former husband, Keith Abel, to attempt to provide explanations. Bakalla's lawyer, James Shapiro, told reporters that she was "an all-American girl from the suburbs." Shapiro said Bakalla lived in fear that Luna would kill her if he believed she had been the one to inform authorities—even if he was in jail. "She may

not have been directly threatened, but she was definitely
afraid," Shapiro told reporters. "She was in fear of her
life. I think she perceived Mr. Luna could get to her from
behind bars." Bakalla, he added, believed that Luna had
friends who were gang members who would have tracked
her down if he thought he had been put behind bars because of her.

And then, he said, she repressed the massacre. "She
knows that it was there subconsciously and she is starting
to explore that now," Shapiro said. "She did not do anything to aid or abet either of the defendants after the
crime. She just kept their secret out of fear for her life for
nine years. I believe the prosecutors in this case recognize
that some people may have legitimate reasons for waiting
before they come forward with information. I would hope
that the public clamor for possible charges of witnesses
would subside not only for the sake of the witnesses in
this case, but also so other potential witnesses in other
cases [feel] comfortable coming forward."

Bakalla had not kept her secret completely to herself.
Before she was married in September 1998, she partially
opened up to Keith Abel, her husband-to-be. "I believe
this was in the context of 'I have a deep dark secret. I'm
about to get married; I shouldn't keep it from you,' " Jerry
Kurz, another of Bakalla's attorneys, told reporters. What
she told Abel was not exactly the truth, though. In her
version, Bakalla merely said she knew the Brown's killers, and did not explain in depth how Luna and Degorski
had shared the details of that night with her. And when
she told him, Abel's reaction had been primarily one of
disbelief, Kurz said. After all, Bakalla and Degorski had
remained friends and Abel had actually met Degorski.
Any immediate concerns Abel might have had were

quelled further because he did not see Degorski act out in any way that might have suggested he was concealing such a secret.

When police reached out to Abel to question him about his knowledge, he was stunned. "He was devastated," one investigator later said. "He had a very difficult time with it."

The backlash, Shapiro disclosed, went beyond the public tongue-lashing. After Bakalla's name surfaced in media reports, she was fired from her job at a suburban restaurant. "She's lost her job over this," he told reporters. "She may have to leave the area. It's ruined her life. It's a feeding frenzy; her family can't stand it. She's a pariah. This is just a normal young woman who happened to know something dangerous that other people didn't know."

Lockett's story emerged through police and her attorney, Kenneth Goff, who said that after she began dating Degorski in high school, he was not only emotionally domineering, but physically abusive. "She said she would wake up each day and basically try to think of how she could avoid making him angry so that she wouldn't be hit," Goff told reporters. "If she said the wrong thing, did the wrong thing, looked the wrong way, things would set him off."

She told authorities that Degorski and Luna tortured small animals and that Degorski kept several knives, including a switchblade and a hunting knife, and a .38-caliber revolver in his basement bedroom, according to the *Chicago Sun-Times*. On one occasion, Degorski had opened the gun and showed her that it was loaded with six bullets. He kept it on a stand next to his bed, she told authorities.

"I would characterize her as a classic abused woman in this relationship," Goff said. Lockett and Degorski broke off the relationship in 1994, he said. For a while, Lockett had a diary in which she had written about the night when Degorski and Luna had recounted the massacre. But eventually, she destroyed it for fear that he might find it. After they broke off, they did not see each other again.

But she was still living in fear, Goff said. In the late 1990s, Degorski tracked down Lockett's mother in Oregon and persuaded her to give him Lockett's telephone number. He telephoned Lockett, and while their conversation was brief and inconsequential, it was a vivid reminder of the secret she had been keeping.

It was Degorski's second attempt to reach out that had triggered Lockett's decision to go to authorities—although months passed before she took action. It began in the fall of 2001 when Degorski telephoned Lockett's mother again, asking for Lockett's telephone number. This time, Lockett's mother called her daughter before giving out the number. Lockett told her mother not to give the number to Degorski, but did not explain why.

That call was unnerving. Degorski, Lockett came to believe, was attempting once more to interject himself in her life in some way. It was then that she began the soul-searching journey that would lead to the arrests. She first told her boyfriend and then they confided in their roommate. Both were so concerned for her safety that they purchased firearm owner's identification cards—a precursor to owning a weapon—but did not purchase any guns. Ultimately, Lockett told her sister, her mother, and finally, Kathleen Parker.

"It took until she finally got into a very strong, supportive network, with friends she can trust and in a relationship with someone she can trust that she finally felt she was able to come forward," Goff told reporters. "She truly is sorry for any pain that she's caused by her silence. She's not this person that just sat on this secret so long out of some sense of loyalty to an old boyfriend. It wasn't that at all. It was a situation where she truly felt fearful and in fear for her life.

"She wants to let the families know that she is sorry and that she is doing everything she can to try and make that right," he said. "Each time this case would resurface, it tore her up because she knew the secret. She saw what these guys did inside that place. Maybe it was selfish, but she thought: *That could happen to me.*"

Lockett, he said, did not view herself as any kind of hero. "She knew it was wrong and it tore her up inside," Goff said. "The longer it went on, the harder it was to ultimately tell."

Luna and Degorski were even more perplexing than Lockett and Luna. Gregg McCrarry, a retired FBI profiler, told the *Daily Herald,* "That's a little bit unusual . . . to do a multiple murder—really a mass murder—and to slide into a normal life . . . to have them just snap out of it and straighten up."

The chance to play God typically doesn't just fade away, he said. "We want murderers to be monsters. We want to be able to know them when we see them. Sometimes you do, but the very unsettling part is sometimes you don't."

"How can a guy kill seven people and be normal?" asked Greg Danielson, co-owner of Gulgren Appliance, where Luna worked six days a week. But it was a question everyone was asking, and not just about Luna, but about

Degorski as well. It was a question asked repeatedly by
police, family members of the victims, and people across
the Chicago area.

Luna's wife, Imelda, who did not even meet Juan until
well after the massacre, was stricken. "He is a quiet guy,"
she told reporters. "To me, he is good. I can assure you
my husband did not do this."

Danielson told reporters, "This is so out of character.
He was a young, responsible family man. Real polite.
Good with customers. Always on time. When we first
heard, we said, 'They've got the wrong guy.' I never even
saw him lose his temper. I never even heard him swear.
He was a very nice guy around here."

Danielson's business partner, Mike Gulgren, also
spoke fondly of Luna to reporters: "He was the kind of
guy that if I needed someone to drive my kids to school,
I'd trust him to do it."

Degorski, though he had a few scrapes with the law
and one serious incident involving his beating of a girlfriend that occurred before the massacre, had, like Luna,
led a relatively nonviolent life.

A woman who was not named told the *Tribune* that
she had met Degorski in the mid-1990s and they had
dated on and off until mid-2001. Never once during that
time, she said, did he so much as hint that he could have
been involved in something of the magnitude of the massacre. "He came into my life as a nice guy," she said. "I
knew him as a different man."

She described Degorski as a man who was not capable
of telling a lie and that he was generous with his time—
the sort of person who would get out of bed in the middle
of the night to rescue a friend whose car had broken
down. She said he liked to go fishing, and because he

always seemed to want to lose weight, he frequently suggested they take bicycle rides or go in-line skating.

After hearing a description of the charges, she said, "I don't know what to think."

By the time of his arrest, Degorski and his brother, Kevin, were living about ten minutes from downtown Indianapolis. Larry Copenhaver, a salesman who had lived next to them, told the *Sun-Times* that they were "nice people." He said Kevin Degorski "was the more responsible one," while "James, he was more laid back, kind of quiet. He was real polite to me. He just kind of fit in with everybody here."

James Blazek, Degorski's boss, told the *Herald* that Degorski was one of his best workers and fit in well with coworkers because he had a good sense of humor and easy manner.

Another neighbor, Dale Bennett, told the *Sun-Times,* "It was quite stunning to us. To be living that close to someone and not really know anything about him—and then come to find out he's involved in, what, seven murders? . . . There was just nothing that would give you the impression anything was wrong."

THIRTY-THREE

I T WAS AN INORDINATELY WARM DAY FOR JANU-
ary, but by nightfall a wickedly icy wind had begun
to invade the village of Palatine. The streets were mostly
empty and those residents venturing outside did so with
their collars turned against the wind.

Christmas decorations still brightened the windows of
some homes, while Christmas trees, robbed of their tinsel
and ornaments and tiny angels, lay along curbsides await-
ing the morning's garbage trucks. High on some of the
light poles along Northwest Highway, imitation candy
canes rustled.

The parking lot of the Eurofresh Market Plaza was less
than one-tenth filled. It is a large parking lot and it is
almost unimaginable that it could ever be completely
filled, even if the stores were giving their goods away.
That evening, the northwest section of the parking lot had
a particularly forlorn look, the asphalt so clean and unmarked that it appeared no one ever parks there.

This was where the Brown's Chicken and Pasta building had once stood and there is little doubt that this space still evokes memories in anyone who has lived in the area for more than a decade. Some will tell you, even now, that the ground is haunted.

It was a few minutes before 9 P.M. on the night of January 8, 2003, almost ten years to the minute since authorities say James Degorski and Juan Luna entered the restaurant and began the forty-four minutes of terror that took seven lives and forever shadowed the lives of surviving family and friends and the community itself.

The arrests of Degorski and Luna brought a moment of relief. But as the realization began to sink in that there would be no quick legal resolution, the familiar frustrations returned: Will this ever end?

ALMOST IMMEDIATELY AFTER DEGORSKI AND LUNA were indicted, prosecutors announced they would seek the death penalty and members of the victims' families said they agreed with the decision. Diane Mennes, the sister-in-law of Thomas Mennes, who began to regularly attend court sessions, said justice could only be served by their execution. "I can't see them sitting in jail and doing their thing and going into the jail yard twice a day," she said. "All the victims are no longer with us."

After Degorski and Luna pleaded not guilty, prosecutors and defense attorneys settled down to what promised to be a lengthy period of pretrial skirmishing over a number of legal issues: an attempt to suppress the defendants' statements, independent DNA testing of the remains of the chicken meal as well as Luna's DNA, and a reexamination of fingerprints lifted from the restaurant. There would be no ballistics tests: Investigators had spent days searching the Fox River for the alleged murder weapon, but it was never found.

Prosecutors disclosed for the first time that in 1998 a man had given a videotaped statement during which he confessed to the murders. While defense lawyers said they intended to explore the alleged confession, prosecutors dismissed the confession as bogus.

"This false claim was thoroughly investigated and discounted," said a spokesman for the Cook County State's Attorney's Office. And a law enforcement official told the *Chicago Tribune* that the man was one of two individuals who claimed they were in the restaurant on the night of the murders, but both men's statements were considered unreliable.

"They would [confess] to anything and everything," the law enforcement source said. Both men had given DNA samples at the time and had been eliminated as suspects when neither of their DNA profiles matched the DNA profile obtained from saliva found on the remains of the chicken meal found in the garbage can in the restaurant.

Luna's attorney, Clarence Burch, announced that he would seek to have the remains of the chicken retested to determine if the first test results, obtained in 1998, were accurate. "We'd like to retest the actual chicken," he said, "but it was a trace amount of DNA to begin with, and we don't know what's left."

At the same time, prosecutors turned over laboratory reports showing that a napkin found with the chicken meal in the garbage contained fingerprints that did not match either Degorski's or Luna's. "The fingerprints did not match anyone in the case," Burch said. "We're using it to negate the presence of my client. They thought this napkin was significant."

Burch said he and Degorski's defense attorney, Mark Levitt, intended to challenge the methods used to collect, store, and test the remains of the chicken. And Levitt steadfastly maintained that his client had not said anything incriminating to the investigators while he was being questioned after his arrest nor was there any physical evidence linking Degorski to the crime.

Prosecutors said that Luna gave a videotaped confession during which he admitted being present during the murders, but placed the blame for the shooting on Degorski. They said that Degorski admitted his role in the crime to his interrogators, but that when the video camera was turned on, he balked and refused to speak further. "It's nothing, there are no confessions or statements," Levitt insisted in court. He added that the tape of Degorski was only a few minutes in length. "And then the taping stopped because there was no point to keep taping and the state stopped it."

In the weeks before the tenth anniversary of the killings, prosecutors gave the defense lawyers computer disks containing nearly 300,000 thousand pages of police reports, interviews, and laboratory reports that had accumulated since the murders occurred. Burch complained that even if he and his staff read a thousand pages a week, digesting the information would take several years. No one expected the trial to begin before sometime late in 2004, if then. The outcome will be up to a judge and jury.

So no one expected there to be a celebration at the site of the killings. Celebrations would have to wait.

But earlier in the day, members of the Castro family had driven to the place where sixteen-year-old Michael Castro had died and placed a wreath there, festooned with seven white ribbons, each carrying the name of one of the victims. Others had anonymously placed candles and a small bouquet nearby.

On that night, it was a sad and shabby memorial, the white ribbons tattered and shredded by the wind, the candles long extinguished. But one could not help but be moved by the gesture, by the realization of all the pain and suffering that took place that night and that has echoed through the lives of the people who loved those who died.

Some family members will tell you that they have felt their dead loved one's spirits, in their hearts always, but in more palpable ways as well, in noises in their homes, in voices in their heads.

A few minutes after 9 P.M. a car pulled into the parking lot and stopped so that the driver had a clear view into the empty space where the Brown's restaurant once stood. The driver, a woman, was alone and she kept her foot on the brake as the motor idled and she stared straight ahead.

Who was she?

It didn't really matter and the moment was not an appropriate one for names and questions, but for quiet respect. The woman appeared to be in her thirties, and an observer might wonder where she was ten years ago on this night, and then be struck by the meaning of that simple number: What is ten years?

Michael Castro would be just a few days away from his twenty-sixth birthday.

Lynn Ehlenfeldt would be fifty-eight, her husband, Richard, fifty-nine.

Thomas Mennes would be forty-two.

Marcus Nellsen would be forty.

Rico Solis would be twenty-seven.

Guadalupe Maldonado would be fifty-six.

It gives one pause: seventy years of life stolen, seventy years of failures and successes, loves and losses, trials and joys, and all of those pleasures large and small that go along with life. Seventy years of ordinary days and special moments snatched away. Seventy years of dreams, stolen.

For one standing in the lot, it seemed as if only a moment had passed, but then it was 9:52 P.M. Ten years ago at that very minute, authorities say, Degorski and Luna walked out of the restaurant, their bloody deed done. Did they ever imagine, one wonders, that a decade later they would find themselves behind bars, fearing the same fate as their victims except at the hands of the state?

ABOUT THE AUTHOR

MAURICE POSSLEY is an award-winning criminal justice reporter for the *Chicago Tribune* with thirty years' experience as a journalist. His investigative reporting has been considered for the Pulitzer Prize on two occasions. Possley is known for his role in breaking the story of the serial killer John Wayne Gacy, who was executed for killing thirty-three people in Chicago, and for his coverage of such high-profile stories as the prosecutions of Timothy McVeigh and Theodore Kaczynski. He has appeared as a legal commentator on NPR and Court TV, and on *Good Morning, America*.